PETER ABELARD:

His Place In History

WITHDRAWN

Kathleen M. Starnes

University Press
of America

To Charlie and Cynthia

ACKNOWLEDGEMENTS

My special thanks and grateful appreciation are due to the professors of the University of Texas at Arlington Department of History; in particular, Dr. Bede Lackner, Dr. E. C. Bock, Dr. Gary D. Stark, and Dr. Arthur W. Tucker; to Ruth Metcalf and the staff of the University of Texas at Arlington Library for their cheerful cooperation and aid in securing texts; to the staff of Southern Methodist University's Bridewell and Fondren Libraries for their help in locating several valuable sources; to Mike Anderson for his help in obtaining a needed text; and to the authors and scholars whose published works I have researched and cited in the bibliography.

June 20, 1980

TABLE OF CONTENTS

Innovations adopted later by the university; students; scholastic method; pagan ethics drawn into theology; a Christian philosophy; later adaptations

PREFACE

There is an inherent difficulty involved in any attempt at determining Abelard's place in history. The problem lies not only in interpreting and understanding his thought, but also in drawing the Abelard of the schools and Christian philosophy away from the popular romantic image of the Abelard whose life was filled with excitement, danger, scandal, tragedy, and defeat. This latter picture of Abelard has resulted in his name, and that of his wife Heloise, being identified as the Romeo and Juliet of twelfth century France. Their names and the story of their tragic love affair have been passed on through the romantic literature of Europe where they are mentioned in the "Roman de la Rose" of William of Loire (c. 1237), Chaucer's <u>Canterbury Tales</u> (c. 1387-1400), Francois Villon's "Ballade des Dames du Temps Jadis" (c. 1461), and Alexander Pope's "Eloisa to Abelard" (1717). But this is not the Abelard who overcame the personal catastrophes of his life to stir the imaginations of his thousands of followers, open their awareness to the power of reason, and instill within their minds a new freedom of thought that could not be eradicated even after he was silenced by the Council of Sens in 1140. This other Abelard, the egocentric, captivating teacher and controversial Christian philosopher--a man who was loyal to his wife in his own fashion but who retained as his first love the excitement of dialectic--is the one who deserves the reverence offered to all the great thinkers of history.

Peter Abelard epitomized the intellectual vitality of the twelfth century renaissance. He

was a master of dialectic who dared to apply Aristotelian logic to both philosophy and theology.
Under his influence and example, Medieval realism
gave way to a modified nominalism, and rationalism was injected into theology. Neither of these
incursions into the realms of Plato and the
Church was welcomed, and thus the man who laid
the foundation for the University of Paris and
provided the impetus for scholasticism became
persecuted by scholars who could not combat his
logic and by theologians who saw his rationalism
as a desecration of faith. Although Abelard was
not so much concerned with the subject matter as
with the excitement of the debate, he nevertheless exercised a profound influence and acted as
a catalyst in the transition of the twelfth century schools of thought from a traditional to an
analytical methodology.

CHAPTER ONE

PETER ABELARD (1079-1142): A BIOGRAPHICAL SKETCH

During 1132 and 1133, Abelard wrote his
Historia Calamitatum in which he sought to com-
fort a troubled friend by a recitation of his own
misfortunes. As an autobiographical work, it was
unique to the Middle Ages in that it was neither
a confession nor a spiritual work, but one which
centered on his life, career, and experiences.
The purpose of the _Historia_ is somewhat suspect
and could have been intended as a publicity
effort to gain sympathy for Abelard to quit the
Abbey of St. Gildas and return to Paris to teach,
which he probably did around 1135. The _Historia_,
and also his correspondence with his wife Heloise,
provide a glimpse into not only the life of the
man, but also into the age in which he lived.
The letters between Abelard and Heloise contain
some discrepancies with respect to the _Historia_,
however, and so are also suspect. They may have
been forged by Jean de Meung in the thirteenth
century as a means for instituting a new rule for
nuns under the name of Abelard. Giles Constable
noted in his _Letters of Peter the Venerable_ that
the rhythmical prose of Heloise's letters to
Abelard is absent from her letters to Peter the
Venerable and there are a number of poorly concluded sentences in her letters.[1] But the evidence is inconclusive, and the letters have not
been completely discredited.[2]

Peter Abelard was "born in a town called Le
Pallet in Brittany near the border about eight
miles . . . east of Nantes,"[3] in 1079. He was
the eldest child of Berengarius who was a member

1

of the minor Breton nobility and served Hoel IV,
Duke of Brittany and Count of Nantes.[4] Abelard's
mother, Lucia, was mentioned briefly in the Historia simply as being very dear to him.[5] There is
documentary evidence in the necrology of the Paraclete, the oratory and later convent established
by Abelard (c. 1129), that he may have had three
brothers named Dagobert, Porcarius, and Radul-
phus. He most likely had only one sister for he
wrote that Heloise "stayed with my sister,"[6]
rather than "one of my sisters" as he referred
once to "one of my brothers."[7] The necrology of
the Paraclete indicates that Abelard had but one
sister named Denise (Dionisia).[8] His own name,
Abaelardus, was possibly a corruption of Habelar-
dus and he used the nickname Bajolardus given him
in his student days.[9] Francois Villon referred
to him in his poem as Esbaillart, but his name in
the vernacular was Abailard or Abelard. For con-
sistency, he will be called Abelard herein.

Abelard's father had gained some degree of
education prior to entering military service and
desired the same for his sons before they followed him in the same career. For Abelard, study
became more important than military glory; so he
renounced his right of inheritance and primogeni-
ture to pursue his education in the field of disputation and logic. In his Historia, he wrote
that he wandered from place to place, and went
"wherever I heard the pursuit of this art was
vigorous."[10] He was fifteen or sixteen when he
departed his father's castle to become a wandering scholar, sometime around 1095. He had received a careful education, but had no talent for
mathematics. Due to his natural inclination,
Abelard concentrated on the trivium of grammar,
logic, and rhetoric, rather than the upper divi-
sion of the seven liberal arts of higher education: the quadrivium of arithmetic, astronomy,
geometry, and music.

Abelard never stated which teachers he sought
out as he wandered, perhaps in order to preserve
the ideas he presented as being totally his own.

But he received some early education from Jean Roscelin (c. 1050-1120), who was a canon (of Compiègne) at Loches in Brittany. Roscelin wrote in a letter that Abelard was his smallest pupil and sat at his feet "from his boyhood to youth," and Otto of Freising (c. 1114-1158) stated that Abelard "had Roscelin for his master."[11] The lecture hall of this famous teacher, who was later condemned for heresy, was at a monastery subject to the Abbey of St. Gildas where Abelard later became Abbot.[12]

About 1100, Abelard arrived in Paris where the great unsolved problem discussed by scholars was that of universals. Under Roscelin's tutelage, Peter Abelard had been exposed to the nominalist viewpoint which denied the reality of abstract ideas and accepted only the concrete individual or object. Once in Paris, Abelard became a student of another famous teacher, William of Champeaux (d. 1121), at the cathedral school of Notre Dame. William had himself studied under Roscelin and also under Anselm of Laon (d. 1117), but preferred the realism of the latter. He taught from the viewpoint based on Plato that the idea was a reality apart from the individuals who constitute it.

Abelard studied under William for a time, but eventually he began to question him and argue against him from a standpoint which was similar to that of Aristotle. Yet, Aristotle's complete works in logic would not become known until the thirteenth century. It was in William's school that Abelard's application of logic to all thought was first manifested. Abelard stated in his Historia that his fellow students considered his conduct improper due to his youth and inexperience. He viewed their attitude as evidence of their jealousy; therefore, he left Paris for Melun with the announced intention of founding his own school.

Abelard may have been around twenty-three years old when he went to Melun. The town was a

royal seat and was situated not far from Paris.[13]
William of Champeaux was displeased with this new
development and attempted, unsuccessfully, to
hinder Abelard's efforts to establish a new
school.   Instead, Abelard stated that his own
"reputation in dialectical skill began to spread"
and that his fame far outshone that of William.[14]
His merciless method of disputation earned him
the nickname of <u>rhinocerus indomitus</u> (wild rhi-
noceros)[15] and his success incited jealousy and
suspicion in the established schools.

     Yet, for all his assertions as to his own
greatness and the demise of William's fame,
Abelard apparently either needed William to maintain his own reputation or else was an exceeding-
ly petty individual, for he transfered his school
from Melun to Corbeil, "nearer to Paris that I
might prove a greater embarrassment."[16]   Abelard
deliberately made a nuisance of himself and then
complained with indignation when his tactics for
gaining attention aroused the anger of those he
taunted.

     Soon after moving to Corbeil, Abelard's
health gave way from overwork--although later
symptoms have prompted the speculation that he
suffered from Hodgkins disease--and he returned
to his home in Brittany.   He remained away from
France for about six years but did not say in his
<u>Historia</u> what he did during this time.   He merely
mentioned that his students "kept eagerly trying
to seek me out."[17]   Significantly, though, when
Abelard finally returned from his lengthy absence,
he sought out his former rival, William of Champeaux who was lecturing on rhetoric, and once
again became his student.   Considering what he
had been through with Abelard a few years before,
William must have been far more patient and
understanding of the exuberance of youth than
Abelard cared to admit.   It would seem from the
sequence of events which followed that Abelard
had returned to William's school not to learn but
to use his teacher once again as a target for his

4

disputatation in order to rebuild his own fame.
His opportunity arose in the controversial issue
of universals.

In his conflict with William over the nature
of universals, Abelard claimed to have won the
debate and to have forced Willaim "by clear proofs
from reasoning to change, yes, to abandon his old
stand on universals."[18] Abelard's natural Aristotelian extension of William's realism had led
to an adroit accusation of pantheism. But Abelard's true skill was in his careful expression;
his greatest concern was in the meaning and proper use of words as the basis of rational understanding, and then, the development of a philosophy of nature or a system of theology would
follow naturally. His own solution to the problem of universals came to be known as conceptualism. Abelard qualified the nominalism of his
early teacher, Roscelin, by considering universals to be judgments rather than mere words.[19]
Universals were concepts formed by the mind when
determining the similarities between perceived
individual objects. The net result of his arguments was that William's lectures fell into dis-
repute while Abelard's teachings gained in pres-
tige and authority.

It was perhaps around 1108 when Abelard took
over the chair of dialectics in the cathedral
school of Paris, which was the very position held
by William when Abelard first became his student.
Robert of Melun (d. 1167) may have been the one
who offered this post to Abelard for he had not
held it long before William made charges against
Robert. He was able to depose Abelard as a
result of this action and replace him with one of
Abelard's rivals; but Abelard wrote that "there
was nothing he could do against me personally."[20]

What followed was a game of Medieval musical
chairs. Abelard departed Paris, leaving his un-
named rival occupying his chair at the cathedral
school, and re-established his school in Melun.
William left Paris for "a certain village outside

5

the city,"[21] and Abelard returned to Paris. He
set up his school on Mount Ste. Geneviève outside
Paris, for it was not yet a part of the city.
William returned to Paris at once "as if to raise
the seige of his soldier whom he had abandoned."[22]
But he only succeeded in taking the teacher's few
students for himself. The rival, then, abandoned
his chair and entered a monastery, probably in
disgust at being made a pawn in such a petty
game. With the excitement of the joust of the
schools being reduced to bickering between the
followers of Abelard and William, Abelard abruptly departed for his home to see his mother into
religious life. He spent two to four years in
Brittany, possibly attending to matters of inheritance with his brothers and sister since his
father had previously entered a monastery. When
he left Brittany, presumably with the chair still
open at Paris and with William now in the see of
Châlons-sur-Marne, Abelard had a clear field in
which to teach philosophy. Instead, he went to
Laon to study divinity under William's former
teacher, Anselm.

Anselm of Laon (1040-1117) had studied under
St. Anselm (d. 1109) and first began teaching in
Paris in 1070 with notable success. His school
of theology, founded in Laon, became the most
famous in Europe. This same Anselm wrote an
interlinear on the scriptures which was used
throughout the Middle Ages. Abelard, however,
considered Anselm to be inept and empty in his
teachings and decided that his studies would
prove fruitless. He attended lectures irregular-
ly and claimed that the other students, who were
offended by his "dispising a man of such renown,"
plotted to make Anselm hostile towards him.[23] It
would seem reasonable to believe that little
prompting would be necessary for a great teacher
to become annoyed with someone who openly demonstrated his contempt for that teacher as Abelard
indicates he did towards Anselm.

Abelard described how he astonished his fellow students with his skill at interpreting the

6

sacred scriptures in a passage of the <u>Historia</u> which was vaguely reminiscent of Luke 2:46-47 in which Christ amazed the doctors with his understanding of the scriptures. Since he had previously only studied philosophical works, his skill at interpretation was received with wonderment and Abelard gave at least three highly successful lectures on "a very obscure passage of the prophet Ezechiel."[24] Abelard felt that his achievement aroused the jealousy of Anselm who forbade him to continue his lectures on the grounds that Abelard's errors might be attributed to Anselm's school. Abelard wrote that the students were "highly indignant at this open manifestation of envy and spite."[25]

It is possible that Abelard unintentionally betrayed his true purpose for seeking out Anselm, as he had William, and then embarking upon a course of behavior which could only serve to antagonize them, when he wrote that "by his persecution, he made me more esteemed."[26] Abelard revealed his motivations, then, and showed himself as not only a master of dialectic, but of manipulation as well. He quickly returned to Paris with his new found notoriety and occupied the chair of dialectics previously given and taken away from him. In Laon remained two of Abelard's rivals, Alberic of Rheims and Lotulph the Lombard, whom Abelard named as the ones who had instigated Anselm against him.[27]

Between 1112 and 1118, Abelard taught at Paris and wrote his <u>Logica Ingredientibus</u> (<u>Logic for Beginners</u>), containing the commentaries on Porphyry in which he argued for dialectics as a major branch of the arts. His annotations to Porphyry and his work, <u>Dialectica</u>, were used as texts. After Anselm's death in 1117, Abelard's fame was unsurpassed in theology as well as in dialectic and rhetoric. Students flocked to Paris from all parts of the civilized world, and Abelard gained wealth and renown in what could be called his personal golden age. The situation changed, however, when Abelard, perhaps bored

7

with his unrivaled success, became involved with a beautiful and talented woman named Heloise.

Heloise--who was under the care of her uncle, a canon named Fulbert--had been brought up and educated in the convent of Argenteuil near Paris.[28] Because Abelard had kept himself aloof from the society of noble women and because he did not wish to become involved with "unclean harlots,"[29] he selected Heloise for her beauty and knowledge of letters to be the object of his deliberate seduction. There was perhaps at first no romantic or idealistic love involved in Abelard's conquest and if the letters attributed to him are not forgeries, he verified this in a letter to Heloise after he had departed from the Abbey of St. Gildas:

> My love, which brought us both to sin,
> should be called lust, not love. I
> took my fill of my wretched pleasures in
> you, and this was the sum total of my
> love.[30]

At first, Abelard arranged to become acquainted with Heloise "through private daily meetings"[31] and then by boarding at the canon's house. Fulbert wanted his niece to receive instruction from the now famous teacher, and so he gave Abelard full charge over Heloise and freedom to instruct her at any time of day or night. His reputation for chastity notwithstanding, even Abelard was astonished by the arrangements:

> I was amazed by his simplicity - if he
> had entrusted a tender lamb to a raven-
> ing wolf it would not have surprised me
> more.[32]

Heloise was receptive to Abelard's advances and, indeed, he was filled with self-confidence due to his fame, youth, and good looks. He was described in the Vita Gosvini by an anonymous author as "fair and of handsome countenance, but slight in build and of short stature."[33]

Abelard's lectures began to suffer, however, as
he found his classes boring and became totally
preoccupied with Heloise and the new-found delight
of love. Abelard resorted to simply repeating
what he had previously taught without the addition
of new thought. His students became disturbed by
his lack of concentration in philosophy, but they
consoled themselves by popularizing the love
verses he created for Heloise.[34]

Several months passed before Fulbert learned
of the affair, and then he separated the lovers.
They continued to meet clandestinely, however,
and were eventually discovered in bed together.
It was shortly after this incident that Heloise
sent a joyful letter to Abelard in which she told
him that she was pregnant and asked what to do.
According to his <u>Historia</u>, Abelard sent her to
Brittany which infers that he remained in Paris.

> I sent her straight to my own country.
> There she stayed with my sister until
> she gave birth to a boy, whom she called
> Astralabe.[35]

Since Abelard discussed Fulbert's quandry as
to how to gain revenge on Abelard without endan-
gering his niece in Brittany, it would appear
that Abelard had remained in Paris and wrote of
Fulbert's grief from first-hand knowledge, rather
than accompanying Heloise to his country. This
sequence of events points out a discrepancy and
reveals a cause for suspecting the later letters
of Abelard and Heloise to be forgeries, since in
one letter Abelard stated:

> You know too how when you were pregnant
> and I took you to my own country you
> disguised yourself in the sacred habit
> of a nun . . . [36]

Surely a dialectician who worried over the precise meanings of words would have taken the care
to use the words which would have conveyed the
proper inferences, for there is a great difference

between "I . . . sent her" and "I took you."
Then, too, the phrase "to my own country" was
used in the Historia and the letters which would
indicate that the writer of the letters lifted
phrases known to have been used by Abelard and
placed them in the letters in order to give a
feeling of authenticity. The phrase also seems
too formal for a personal letter when a more
direct expression could have been used, such as
"to Brittany," or "to my sister's house."

After Heloise had left Paris, her uncle was
unconsolable and Abelard began to feel guilt and
remorse for his actions, and sought to make
amends. He visited Fulbert and, after first reminding the girl's uncle that "since the beginning
of the human race women had brought the noblest
men to ruin,"[37] he offered to secretly marry
Heloise. Fulbert agreed to the plan "and sealed
the reconciliation . . . with a kiss."[38] This
may have been more of a literary device to prepare the reader for a Judas-like betrayal than an
actual incident. Abelard then went to Brittany
to fetch his mistress.

Heloise objected to the arrangement, however, and Abelard listed her reasons in the
Historia as based on the risk involved, for she
did not believe a secret wedding would appease
her uncle, and on the disgrace the marriage
would bring upon Abelard. Her arguments against
a philosopher having a family were carefully detailed in the Historia, but they also appear in
other of Abelard's works written prior to the
Historia.[39]

After their son was born, Heloise and Abelard left him with Abelard's sister; they returned to Paris and were quietly married. No
clear reason was given by Abelard for the necessity of secrecy, but one could speculate that he
desired to legitimize his son, or that he did not
wish to jeopardize his career in the Church, or
that he did not want to be compared with incon-
tinent clerics; but in a letter to Heloise

10

attributed to Abelard, he stated that he married her "to keep you whom I loved beyond measure for myself alone."[40] It was in this same letter that Abelard identified his love as lust. He most likely married Heloise, then, because of a possessive jealousy.

At the time of their marriage, Abelard was a canon, but when he became one and of what church is unknown; but Heloise was said to have asked Abelard, as stated in the Historia, ". . . what should you, a cleric and canon, do to avoid base pleasure to sacred duties . . ."[41] It is also possible that there were two classes of secular canons, other than the Canons Regular who were celibate, one composing a Cathedral Chapter and the other not.[42]

After they were wed, Abelard and Heloise "saw each other only rarely and then on the quiet,"[43] but the uncle spread the news of their marriage despite his previous promise to Abelard. Heloise responded by cursing and swearing that it was a lie. Fulbert became abusive and Abelard secretly removed Heloise from her uncle's house to the convent of Argenteuil where she was clothed in a nun's habit except for the veil. When he discovered what had happened, Fulbert assumed that Abelard was ridding himself of his wife and, with his supporters, he formed a plan for revenge which resulted in Abelard being castrated one night as he slept in an inner room of his lodgings. Two of the conspirators were captured and were similarly mutilated and had their eyes put out.[44]

In his Historia, Abelard stated that the mutilation came "quickly and suddenly when I was asleep and so felt little pain."[45] Instead, it was the shame that tormented Abelard. He worried about being subjected to insults and derision and so he fled, as it were, to the Abbey of St. Denis in Paris to escape the pity and loud lamentations of the crowds that gathered at his house:

11

> . . . it was . . . confusion springing
> from shame rather than devotion the
> result of conversion, which drove me
> to the refuge of monastic cloister.[46]

By his replies to the later letters of Heloise, reminding him of the love they had shared, Abelard's affection seemed to abruptly cease. Instead, he appeared annoyed by her insistence on dwelling on the past, and finally demanded that she drop the subject and adjust to the situation.

Both Abelard and Heloise (who may have been nineteen years old at the time) entered religious life shortly after Abelard fled to St. Denis. In one of the letters attributed to Heloise written to Abelard, she mentioned, with some degree of resentment, that she took her vows before her husband:

> . . . perhaps you were thinking how
> Lot's wife turned back. . . . Your
> lack of trust in me over this one
> thing, I confess, overwhelmed me with
> grief and shame.[47]

She entered the convent of Argenteuil and Abelard entered the Benedictine monastery of St. Denis.

While it might appear that neither Heloise nor Abelard seemed particularly concerned about their child, it was not unusual during the Middle Ages for people to give up everything and enter religious life, even to the extent that parents would give their children to relatives. Guibert, Abbot of Nogent (1064?-1125), as an example, was in this manner "abandoned" by his mother when he was twelve years old. Heloise mentioned her son in a later letter to Peter the Venerable when asking for a favor in finding the young man a prebend, and Abelard sent him some verses of advice around 1135 when their son was perhaps seventeen years old.[48] This could be interpreted to show that Astralabe's parents at least kept track of him, perhaps through correspondence with Abelard's

12

relatives.

Abelard's reputation was not damaged by his mutilation, but instead his fame increased and he was encouraged to resume his teaching by the clerks who declared, as Abelard stated in the Historia, that:

> . . . the hand of the Lord had touched me for the express purpose of freeing me from the temptations of the flesh and the distractions of the world so that I could devote myself to learning and thereby prove myself a true philosopher not of the world but of God.[49]

Abelard may have regretted his rash act of entering the monastery before finding out whether or not he had lost the respect of his students, for after they began pressing him and the Abbot of St. Denis for Abelard to continue his lectures, he embarked upon a campaign destined to make himself unpopular with the resisdents of St. Denis and lay the way clear for his departure.

The method used by Abelard was the same as he had used with William of Champeaux and Anselm of Laon. He used Abbot Adam and the monks of St. Denis as opponents to deride. He spoke out "both in public and private against their intolerable irregularities,"[50] and ignoring his own faults and past indiscretions, he became a champion for morality and celibacy. Abelard made no mention of any subsequent conversion in his Historia after his initial explanation for why he entered St. Denis, and there is little evidence to support Abelard's sharp condemnation of his fellow monks. It would appear that his motive for his lambasts against the monks may be quite literally taken when he wrote in the Historia:

> I . . . made myself such a burden and nuisance to them all that they gladly seized on the daily importunities of my pupils as a pretext for having me

13

removed from their midst. . . . and
I retired to a priory where I could
devote myself to teaching as before.[51]

Abelard emerged from the monastery of St. Denis with his powers enhanced and once again his
fame spread throughout Europe. He withdrew with
his students to the priory of St. Ayoul in Provins, which was about twenty-five miles east of
Melun in the territory of Theobald, Count of
Troyes and Champagne, and of Blois and Chartres.
There Abelard taught both sacred scripture and
philosophy, with the result that his school drew
crowds of students from other schools and, as he
saw it, again brought the envy and hatred of
other teachers to him. Interestingly enough, he
became an advocate for the Christian philosophy
of Origen at this time; Origen was also castrated,
albeit by his own hand.

Two people--unnamed by Abelard but possibly
Alberic and Lotulph--constantly "pressed persons
prominent in religion" to forbid him to teach.[52]
The objections raised were such as to exclude all
areas of teaching to Abelard. On the one hand,
it was said that a monk should not teach secular
literature, but on the other hand he had not
studied the Sacred Science under a master and,
therefore, should not teach that subject either.
Abelard incited further controversy when he composed a theological tract, De unitate et Trinitate
divina (On the Unity and Trinity of God) (c. 1118-
1121), in which he exponded on the subject using
a rational and philosophical approach instead of
a theological approach based in faith. Abelard
said:

> . . . it is ridiculous for a man to pro-
> claim to others what neither he nor his
> pupils can grasp by their intelligence.[53]

Since William of Champeaux and Anselm of Laon were
dead, it fell to Alberic and Lotulph to call for
a council against Abelard, and thus the Council
of Soissons came to be convened in 1121.

14

Abelard was accused of having written that there were three Gods, but, as he pointed out, his judges in the matter were also his rivals and accusers. The fact that Abelard's treatise was the last business brought before the council would indicate that it had not been called specifically against Abelard as he inferred in his <u>Historia</u>: "Then my rivals . . . got a Council to meet against me . . . "[54] In fact, the Council of Soissons legislated in a number of matters, including the non-validity of a Mass said by a married priest. But Abelard restated in his <u>Historia</u> that the council was meant specifically for him when he said that they,

> . . . had a long conference on what was to be decreed regarding me and my book which was the question especially for which they had been convened.[55]

Again, Abelard drew a scriptural comparison between himself and Christ when he paraphrased in his <u>Historia</u> the section from John 7:25-26 concerning his speaking publicly on his position daily before the council was seated. The Biblical verses,

> But lo, he speaketh boldly, and they say nothing unto him. Do the rulers know indeed this is the very Christ?[56]

became in Abelard's <u>Historia</u>:

> Behold now he speaks openly and no one utters a word against him . . . Do the judges recognize that they and not he are wrong?[57]

Since his rivals could not dispute against Abelard, they convinced Conon, Bishop of Praeneste and Legate of Pope Calixtus II, to ignore the advice for caution given by Bishop Geoffrey of Chartres, and to condemn the book without an inquiry. The basis for the condemnation was not the content of the tract, but that it had been

15

publicly read and distributed without Papal or
other ecclesiastical authority. Abelard was required to burn his book before the council, re-
cite the Athanasian Creed, and be "confined to
perpetual enclosure in a different monastery."[58]
Abbot Geoffrey of St. Medard took Abelard to his
Cluniac cloister, which Abelard equated to being
dragged off to prison. The monks of St. Medard
joyously received the famous teacher, but Abelard
brooded over the possible damage wrought upon his
reputation by the council. The judgement of the
Council of Soissons was contrary to ecclesiastical law, and the ensuing public outcry led to
Abelard's release from St. Médard within a few
days. He was then returned to St. Denis by the
legate, but Abelard considered the monks there to
be his enemies since his previous criticisms of
their manner of living had antagonized them.

Once he was back at St. Denis, Abelard again
began to incite the monks against himself by re-
proving them for "their base life and shameless
conduct."[59] He finally managed after a few
months to provoke them into taking action against
him when he asserted that Dionysius the Areopag-
ite, who had been converted by St. Paul, and St.
Denis of Paris, who was the patron saint of the
abbey and of France, were not the same person as
alleged by the monks of the abbey. Abelard expressed a naive horror in his Historia--which was
inconsistent with his great intellect--that they
should become angered and threatened to take him
before the king for demeaning their patron saint
"as one who would take from him the glory and
crown of his kingdom."[60] This was more than
Abelard had expected, and when they refused to
give him some punishment according to their rule
but insisted on holding him to go before the king,
Abelard secretly fled the abbey, with the assistance of some of his followers, and took refuge
at the priory of St. Ayoul.

Shortly thereafter, Abbot Adam happened to
visit the priory while on his way to see Count
Theobald on business. The prior asked the abbot

16

to absolve Abelard and allow him to leave St. Denis, but the abbot demanded that Abelard return at once lest the prior and Abelard both be excommunicated. The prior had, after all, harbored a fugitive monk. A few days later, Abbot Adam died and was succeeded by the great Abbot Suger.

Abelard appealed first to Suger, who would not agree to release him from St. Denis, and then to the king, Louis VI, through his seneschal Stephen de Garlande. The matter was resolved in Abelard's favor with the requirement that he could not become subject to another abbey. Abelard claimed that Suger did not want the monastery to lose "the renown it enjoyed through me,"[61] but considering that Abelard had consistently denounced the monks and had disputed the authenticity of their patron saint, it would seem that the "renown" was mostly infamous.

Instead, it seems reasonable to believe that Abbot Suger did not want to set a precedent by allowing a monk to renounce one monastery for another at will. Certainly, the abbot may have desired to retain the noted teacher, but the issue involved was also one of discipline. The monasteries sought, if anything, to teach Abelard humility by insisting that he not be treated in a special manner and not be granted rights and privileges not accorded to others. However, to Abelard, who had no true vocation for religious life, this amounted to persecution.

Abelard, then, with the permission of Abbot Suger, departed St. Denis and, with the approval of Bishop Hato, built an oratory of reeds and thatch on a plot the bishop gave him in the wilderness of the diocese of Troyes. He named his small chapel the Holy Trinity and lived a hermit-like existence with only the company of one of his clerks. It did not take long for his students to discover his whereabouts, and they "built themselves . . . huts on the banks of the Ardusson, and looked like hermits rather than scholars."[62] Abelard resumed teaching the crowds of students who came and his rivals realized that their actions had only served to increase Abelard's fame. The students provided for Abelard's daily needs and enlarged his oratory in wood and stone. He renamed the building the Paraclete (Comforter) and thus managed, in one easy stroke, to rekindle controversy around himself.

In his <u>Historia</u>, Abelard indicated that he was totally surprised by the reaction against this choice of names for his oratory. But his complaints ring hollow, for he would infer that while he was shrewd enough to find arguments against well-established custom, he was also naive enough to be shocked at an antagonistic response when he broke with that custom. Instead, the use of the name of the Paraclete afforded Abelard with an opportunity to demonstrate his ability at disputation by defending his choice of the name associated with the Third Person of the Trinity. Significantly, the people who first "strongly blamed" him were some of his followers.[63]

The objections voiced by some of his students presented Abelard with the chance to enumerate the differences,

> . . . between the Paraclete and the Paraclete, the Spirit . . . just as the Trinity and each person of the Trinity is called God and the helper, so too is the term Paraclete, that is comforter, correctly applied . . . [64]

Nevertheless, Abelard went on to say in his arguments that the Holy Spirit had the right to claim a temple dedicated to Him.

Abelard continued to dwell at the oratory and his fame spread throughout the world. This prompted his former adversaries to stir up against him those whom Abelard termed "some new Apostles," and whom have often been identified as St. Norbert and St. Bernard.[65] This, however, is debatable since there are no available sermons of St.

Norbert containing an attack on Abelard, and St. Bernard's criticisms came after the <u>Historia Calamitatum</u> was written.[66]

With the assumption that Abelard had meant St. Norbert and St. Bernard in his complaint of the "new apostles . . . (who) went up and down the countryside and in their preaching shamelessly kept backbiting"[67] him, Abelard's complaint could be interpreted as an attempt to set the stage for a new focus for his disputation. He wrote the <u>Historia</u> while contemplating his departure from St. Gildas, and with William of Champeaux and Anselm of Laon deceased and his two rivals, Alberic and Lotulph, being too insignificant, it is possible that he had turned his attention to using Bernard of Clairvaux as his means for demonstrating his debating skills and quickly regaining any fame he may have lost while dwelling in the far reaches of Brittany. If this was the case, it was definitely a tactical mistake, for Bernard was a spiritual mystic rather than a philosopher, and Abelard was unable in the end to stand against the sheer determination and faith of Bernard with only the tools of dialectic. When Bernard refused later to enter the arena of philosophical debate, Abelard gave up the dialectic approach with him and turned instead to Rome with the hope of finding a receptive audience. Bernard's refusal to play the philosophical game of mental gymnastics was what brought Abelard to his eventual defeat.

Abelard began showing signs of paranoia towards the end of his stay at the Paraclete, and he attributed his rising fear of persecution to the preaching of the two "new apostles,"

> . . . whenever I learned of a meeting
> of ecclesiastics, I supposed it was to
> condemn me.[68]

But other than his statement of his fear, Abelard makes no mention of concrete reasons for that fear. No one had forbidden him to teach and he

19

had not been threatened with a council. Indeed,
his primary problem may have been that he was
being left alone and he could not find self-ful-
fillment without being involved in controversy.
He needed an opponent. At the same time, however,
his pupil Hilary suggested in his Lament that the
school at the Paraclete was closed due to the
large numbers of unruly students.[69]

Sometime between 1118 and 1125, Abelard became a priest, for in 1125 he was elected to be
Abbot of the monastery of St. Gildas de Rhuys in
the diocese of Vannes in Brittany, and he quickly
accepted the post. He stated in his Historia that
he was actually feeling the envy of the French,
and then he termed Brittany as

> . . . a barbarous country . . . (in
> which he) did not know the language
> . . . and (that) the people of that
> country were rude and uncultured.[70]

It should be remembered, however, that Abelard
grew up in Brittany, had studied under Roscelin
there, had returned there at least three times,
and had left his son there to be raised by his
sister. Even his father and mother had entered
religious life in Brittany. Abelard complained
that he could not speak the language, but even
granting that there were several dialects in
Brittany, he lived there at St. Gildas for ten
years and could have gained some proficiency
during that time. Yet, it was his way to com-
plain and bemoan his fate rather than use his intellect for constructive and practical work.

The monks of St. Gildas he described as base
and incorrigible with a reputation known to all,
but he went there to be their abbot because he
feared to remain in France. Once at the monastery, Abelard began to insist that the monks give
up their concubines and children and submit to
discipline. Since he himself had given up his
wife only due to unfortunate circumstance and had
never shown any regard for discipline in his own

20

dealings with the abbey of St. Denis, it should have come as no surprise to Abelard that the monks of St. Gildas would not be eager to follow his instructions in these matters. Instead, the monks turned against him so that Abelard wrote:

> . . . I felt certain that if I tried to force them to the life of rule to which they had been professed, it would be at the cost of my life; and yet if I did not do it to the best of my power, I would be damned.[71]

It was ironic that after having given so much trouble to Abbots Adam and Suger, Abelard found himself at last in their position.

Abelard began to feel that he was being useless and that his life at St. Gildas was fruitless to himself as well as to everyone else. He worried about the oratory he had abandoned, but then Abbot Suger provided a solution to the matter by confiscating the abbey at Argentuil and expelling the community of nuns which included their prioress Heloise.

When Abelard learned about the fate of Heloise and her followers in 1128, he returned to France to invite them to take over the oratory. He gave it, and all the property connected with it, to the nuns, and on November 28, 1131 Pope Innocent II confirmed the donation in perpetuity. Heloise found fame at the Paraclete and she was admired for

> . . . her spirit of religion, her prudence and her great meekness in every circumstance, a virtue inseparable from patience.[72]

Because the neighbors of the nuns found fault with Abelard for not taking better care of the sisters, he began to visit them "quite often to help them in any way I could."[73] He decided to provide for the nuns as best he could and to be

with them personally so that they would rever him
and he could attend to their needs. Due to the
persecutions from the monks of St. Gildas, Abelard
returned to the Paraclete frequently and, consequently, he considered them to be "a haven of
peace from this stormy tempest."[74] It would seem
reasonable to believe that Abelard remained absent from St. Gildas as much as possible. He was
in France on January 20, 1131 when Pope Innocent
II consecrated the high altar at the Benedictine
abbey of Morigny near Etampes. Abelard had gone
to the ceremony to request the papal legate,
Geoffrey of Lèves, Bishop of Chartres, to be sent
to St. Gildas. It was at Morigny that Abelard
met Bernard of Clairvaux for the first time.[75]

    Abelard's frequent visits to the Paraclete,
which he stated were in response to public criticism on his absence, resulted in new criticism
for his presence there. Gossip abounded to the
effect that he:

            . . . was still in the power of a
            lingering delight in carnal lust
            and could scarcely or never endure
            the absence of (his) old lover.[76]

Abelard marveled at the accusation and remarked
that since he had not "the power to commit base
acts, how is it that suspicion remains?"[77]

    Since it is possible that Abelard wrote his
Historia to gain sympathy for his leaving St.
Gildas to teach again in Paris, it is also possible that he took care to prepare the way so that
he would not be expected to remain at the Paraclete either. His description of the criticism
for not visiting the Paraclete and the gossip
aroused by his subsequent calls on the nuns could
have been an exaggeration to excuse his later
abandonment of the oratory.

    In his Historia, Abelard discussed several
attempts made on his life by the unruly monks of
St. Gildas. They tried to poison him twice, once

22

putting it in the chalice used during Mass and later by putting it in his food when he visited one of his brothers; but in the latter instance, another monk was inadvertently killed. The monks went so far in their aggression against their abbot that Abelard at last excommunicated them. They, in turn, hired brigands to murder him whenever they thought he would be traveling away from the abbey.

Other monks he compelled to publicly swear that they would leave the abbey, but even in this they defied him,

> . . . until finally by authority of the Roman Pontiff through a special legate they were compelled in the presence of the count and some bishops, to give an oath regarding this and many other matters.[78]

Once the legate departed, however, the monks were again rebellious to the point of drawing a sword to Abelard's throat so that he escaped only with an escort from the temporal prince, probably Conon IV, Duke of Brittany.

Abelard concluded his _Historia Calamitatum_ around 1133 to 1135, and it was shortly thereafter that he fled the abbey of St. Gildas for Paris. It is probable that he and Heloise did not meet again after he went to Paris since he commenced to send written material to the nuns at the Paraclete and began them with letters to Heloise. By 1136, Abelard was again successfully lecturing to crowds of students on Mount Ste. Geneviève. He left St. Gildas with the consent of his bishop and the right to retain his rank as abbot. According to John of Salisbury in his _Metalogicon_, Abelard left Paris in 1136, and until the Council of Sens in 1140, there are no records indicating his whereabouts. It is most likely, however, that Abelard must have remained in or near Paris since he was attacked at the Council of Sens for the corrupting influence of his teachings in theology.

In 1139, William of St. Thierry--who had
known Abelard personally and who was also a good
friend of Bernard of Clairvaux--read Abelard's
Theologia, which was a rewritten and expanded
version of the previously condemned tract, De
unitate et Trinitate divina. William of St.
Thierry found thirteen heretical points in the
Theologia and he listed them with his refutations
in a statement which he sent to Bernard and to
Bishop Geoffrey of Chartres. Bernard twice went
to Abelard on the matter and tried to convince him
to restate his views along more traditional lines,
but to no avail. It is quite possible that
Bernard saw Abelard's rationalism on sacred subjects as an affront to pure faith, but he gave
Abelard several opportunities for reconciliation. Abelard, who had felt persecuted at the
Paraclete where there was no threat of danger,
now ignored the danger signals and stood firm in
his belief that clear thinking was an aid to faith,
while Bernard contended that faith transcended
thought.

Bernard appealed to the Bishop of Sens, and
then to the Bishop of Paris to obtain permission
to preach to Abelard's students. Abelard's response was to bring out a fourth edition of his
Theologia, unchanged in all essentials. When the
new treatise came out, Bernard then sent an appeal to the Pope with a treatise against Abelard's
heresies. After the Council of Sens in 1140, he
also wrote harsh and inflammatory letters to the
cardinals at Rome, but then, Bernard was well
aware of Abelard's talent for speech and he apparently did not want to indulge in a lengthy debate.
To Bernard, it was not a matter of verbal skill or
mental adroitness, but a matter of saved or lost
souls--a matter of Heaven or Hell, life or death--
and such a serious issue did not warrant verbal
pleasantries.

Abelard was the one who, in June 1140, asked
Archbishop Henry of Sens to arrange a meeting between himself and Bernard of Clairvaux. His intention was to engage Bernard in a public disputa-

24

tion on their disagreements. At first, Bernard refused to attend because he believed that he would be no match for the famous dialectician and because he did not approve of arguing over faith. His friends persuaded Bernard to change his mind and meet with Abelard, but instead of disputation, Bernard cut directly to the heart of the matter. He wrote to and met with the bishops who were to sit at the Council of Sens, and he preached publicly before his meeting with Abelard on what he considered Abelard's heresies and won the support of the public and the bishops even before the council had met. John of Salisbury and Berengar of Poitiers both wrote of a meeting prior to the council wherein the bishops condemned Abelard's theological writings in his absence. The bishops, themselves, mentioned the meeting in their account to the pope of the Council's findings.

When Abelard arrived at the council prepared for a disputation, he found himself in the position of defendant at an ecclesiastical council. Bernard read aloud a list of Abelard's heresies and called upon Abelard either to deny the charges or to prove or correct the views contained in the Theologia. Abelard did not make any complaint against his treatment at the council or the integrity of the council, but neither did he offer to defend himself. Instead, Abelard refused to reply to the accusation and said that he would appeal to the pope directly.

Abelard may have feared another Council of Soissons, or he may have felt that the large social occasion which included the king and Count Theobald, to be inappropriate for a dissertation on theological subtleties. Nevertheless, the council sent a report of the events to Pope Innocent II and informed him that they had agreed to condemn Abelard as a heretic, and Bernard endorsed this by also writing to the pope requesting that a sentence of excommunication be passed on Abelard. The pope confirmed the sentence and had Abelard's books burnt at St. Peter's in Rome.[79]

Without waiting to hear of the council's actions, Abelard began his overland journey to Rome to make his appeal. He paused along his route at the abbey of Cluny where he was made welcome and encouraged to rest awhile by the abbot, Peter the Venerable. The Abbot of Citeaux, Rainald, arrived about that time and Peter advised Abelard to return with him to settle his differences with Bernard. This was, in fact, accomplished at the abbey of Citeaux through the mediation of Abbot Rainald, and then Abelard returned to Cluny. Peter the Venerable sent a letter, along with Abelard's written confession of faith, to Pope Innocent II in July 1140 requesting permission for the teacher to remain at Cluny as a monk since Bernard had been placated:

> He . . . told us that through the mediation of the abbot of Citeaux he had made his peace with the abbot of Clairvaux and that their previous differences were settled. Meanwhile, . . . he decided to abandon the turmoil of schools and teaching and to remain in your house of Cluny.[80]

The pope lifted the sentence and Abelard spent the last eighteen months of his life at Cluny and the sister-house of St. Marcel at Chalon, where he went for rest and the mild climate during his last illness.

Abelard wrote an _Apologia_ for Bernard, but it was not a retraction nor was it written in the spirit of a penitent, but rather as one who had been misunderstood and wronged. The tone of the _Apologia_ is not so sharp as in Abelard's other writings, for he was sixty-one years old and in ill health, but he clung to his standard of ethics and rational faith even though he was no longer eager to engage in verbal battles. He concluded his _Apologia_ by stating:

> My friend has concluded his list of errors with the remark: 'They are

found partly in Master Peter's book
of theology, partly in his Sentences,
and partly in his Scito te Ipsum.'
But I have never written a book of
Sentences, and therefore the remark
is due to the same malice or ignorance as the errors themselves.[81]

Bernard had won a triumph inasmuch as Abelard
was silenced, but his own tactics were viewed in a
critical light by several contemporary writers,
including Otto of Freising and John of Salisbury.
Abelard, meanwhile, rewrote his treatise on dialectics for his brother Dagobert and Astralabe.
Abelard wrote in a letter to Heloise that was preserved by one of his students, Berengar of Poitiers:

. . . logic has made me hated by the
world. For the perverted . . . say
that I am supreme as a logician, but
am found wanting in my understanding
of Paul. They proclaim the brilliance
of my intellect but detract from the
purity of my Christian faith . . . I
do not wish to be a philosopher if it
means conflicting with Paul, nor to be
an Aristotle if it cuts me off from
Christ.[82]

He also wrote at Cluny his Monitum (Reminders) to
Astralabe, as well as his Dialogus inter Philosophum, Judaeum et Christianum (Dialogue Between a
Philosopher, a Jew and a Christian), the latter
being a restatement on ethics.[83]

Peter described Abelard's life at Cluny as
saintly, humble, and devoted. Abelard lived on
the barest necessities and spent his time reading,
praying, writing, and composing. Perhaps it was
at Cluny that Abelard at last became converted to
the religious life of a monk. When Abelard became
"more troubled than usual from skin irritation and
other physical ailments,"[84] Peter sent him to take
the milder climate at the priory of St. Marcel for

a rest. Abelard died there on April 21, 1142 after confessing his sins and taking Communion. Peter granted him absolution from his sins and secretly took his body to the Paraclete for burial.

Abelard's many works provide a glimpse into the daily life and routine of the twelfth century schools. His treatises on logic and universals consist mostly of commentaries on the works of Porphyry and Boethius as is the case with Logica Ingredientibus (Logic for Beginners) and Nostrorum petitioni sociorum (Written in Response to the Request of Our Friends), and are valuable source documents for the philosophical interests of the early twelfth century as Abelard carefully described the theories which he vigorously attacked. The problem with dating Abelard's works is that he rarely dated anything he wrote, and references within a work to known events must be checked to derive a fair approximate time. The net result is that little has been dated, and the dates assigned to most of his works are subject to interpretation.

His Dialectica was a logical work probably written prior to 1125. In addition to this, he wrote Scito te Ipsum (Know Thyself), in which he favored the rule of conscience over the letter of the law. His Sic et Non (Yes and No) contained some 156 problems in which contradictory statements from the Bible and writings of the Church Fathers were listed without any solution being provided. This work was used as a teaching manual for disputation and to stimulate his students to use their minds in seeking the truth.

De unitate et Trinitate divina (On the Unity and Trinity of God) was composed between 1118 and 1121, and was burned at the Council of Soissons in 1121. Abelard rewrote and expanded this work in his Theologia Christiana (Christian Theology) and later planned a comprehensive three part Theologia. It was the Introductio (Introduction) from the Theologia which first caught the attention of William of St. Thierry. Abelard also wrote the

Expositio in epistula ad Romanos (Commentary on St. Paul's Letter to the Romans) and a commentary on the six days of creation entitled Expositio in Hexameron, possibly around 1135, for the nuns of the Paraclete. In response to requests from Heloise, Abelard composed 34 short sermons and a number of hymns and prayers for the sisters.

The Historia Calamitatum may have been written between 1132 and 1133, although it could have been as late as 1135. Abelard left St. Gildas probably towards the end of 1135 for he was teaching in Paris by 1136. Opinions also vary on when he wrote his lengthy letter in verse, the Monitum, giving advice to Astralabe, and the date is cited as early as 1135 or as late as 1141. The Apologia was written at Cluny and is a rebuttal to Bernard's accusations. Also written at Cluny was the unfinished Dialogus inter Philosophum, Judaeum et Christianum, which was intended to be his chief book on ethics.[85]

The Letters of Abelard and Heloise are possible forgeries, written in the thirteenth century by Jean de Meung to justify the last letter which prescribes a new, more lenient rule for nuns.

It is difficult to assess the historical impact of Peter Abelard. His logical writings were not copied after the thirteenth century and he left no school associated with his name. But he had a profound influence on philosophy and education, nevertheless, for Abelard--who was one of the truly brilliant and original thinkers of his time--was the vanguard for the transition in Medieval thought which led to Scholasticism, with its use of scriptural and patristic quotes, and eventually to the Enlightenment. Abelard had much to do with the abandonment of Plato in favor of Aristotle, and the main reason why his own idea of conceptualism as the solution to the nature of universals did not endure was because Aristotle's solution was discovered; yet, the two conclusions were remarkably similar.

Abelard was a direct influence in the subesquent rejection of the mystic attitude and the adoption of one which may be called rationalistic. His analytical method and persistent criticism of the meaning of words were distinctive characteristics of his style of philosophy, and his dialectical method became a model for future generations to build upon.

CHAPTER ONE FOOTNOTES

[1]Peter the Venerable, The Letters of Peter the Venerable, ed. Giles Constable with introduction and notes, vol. 2 (Cambridge, Massachusetts: Harvard University Press, 1967), p. 38, from the Introduction.

[2]Peter and Heloise Abelard, The Letters of Abelard and Heloise, trans. Betty Radice (New York: Penguin Books, 1976), pp. 47-48. Great detail on the possible system of forgeries is discussed on p. 48, n.2.

[3]Peter Abelard, The Story of Abelard's Adversities, A Translation with Notes of the Historia Calamitatum, trans. J. T. Muckle with a preface by Étienne Gilson (Toronto, Canada: The Pontifical Institute of Mediaeval Studies, 1964), p. 11, Hist. Cal. Le Pallet is actually closer to "twelve miles east and a little south of Nantes." This book will be referred to in future footnotes by the name of the translator, and the notation, Hist. Cal., will be used to indicate that the information cited from the paper is derived from Abelard's Historia Calamitatum.

[4]Joseph McCabe, Peter Abelard (New York: G. P. Putnam's Sons, 1901), p. 6.

[5]Muckle, Adversities, Hist. Cal., p. 20.

[6]Ibid., p. 30.

[7]Abelard, The Letters of Abelard and Heloise, trans. Radice, p. 103.

31

[8]Ibid., p. 57.

[9]Peter Abelard, The Story of My Misfortunes, The Autobiography of Peter Abelard, trans. Henry Adams Bellows with an introduction by Ralph Adams Cram (New York: Macmillan Publishing Company, Inc., 1922), p. 81. This book will be referred to in future footnotes by the name of the translator.

[10]Muckle, Adversities, Hist. Cal., p. 12.

[11]McCabe, Peter Abelard, p. 10.

[12]Ibid., pp. 10-11. McCabe interprets Roscelin's "Locensis ecclesia" to mean the monastery at Locmenach in Brittany.

[13]Muckle, Adversities, p. 13. Muckle gives 1102 for the year of his opening the school at Melun since it is known that Philip I was in Paris in the summer of 1102 and in Bourges in October 1102, and Melun lies between. Although Abelard does not state that Philip intervened against William, he does speak of "some men of influence" on whose help he relied. Hist. Cal., p. 14.

[14]Ibid., Hist. Cal., p. 14.

[15]Meyrick Heath Carré, Realists and Nominalists (London: Oxford University Press, 1961), p. 42.

[16]Muckle, Adversities, Hist. Cal., p. 14.

[17]Ibid., p. 15.   [18]Ibid., p. 16.

[19]Carré, Realists and Nominalists, p. 63.

[20]Muckle, Adversities, Hist. Cal., p. 18.

[21]Ibid., p. 19. [22]Ibid. [23]Ibid., p. 21.

[24]Ibid., p. 23. [25]Ibid., p. 24. [26]Ibid.

[27]Ibid. Muckle states in his footnote that

Alberic eventually became Archbishop of Bourges in
1137, but that there is little known of Lotulphus.

[28]Ibid., Hist. Cal., p. 38. Muckle notes that
Heloise's mother is listed in the necrology of the
Paraclete as Hersinde, but her father's name is
not known.

[29]Ibid., Hist. Cal., p. 25.

[30]Abelard, The Letters of Abelard and Heloise,
trans. Radice, p. 153. Letter 4, Abelard to
Heloise.

[31]Ibid., Hist. Cal., p. 66. [32]Ibid., p. 67.

[33]J. G. Sikes, Peter Abailard (Cambridge: The
University Press, 1932; reprint ed., New York:
Russell and Russell, Inc., 1965), p. 6.

[34]Muckle, Adversities, Hist. Cal., p. 29.

[35]Abelard, The Letters of Abelard and Heloise,
trans. Radice, p. 69. There has been no explanation for the choice of the unusual name of Astralabe or Astrolabe. To be consistent, Abelard's
son will be referred to as Astralabe, as does
Radice.

[36]Ibid., p. 146. Letter 4, Abelard to Heloise.

[37]Ibid., Hist. Cal., p. 70. [38]Ibid.

[39]Ibid., p. 73. This is derived from the
findings of J. T. Muckle and T. P. McLaughlin,
Mediaeval Studies, vol. XII, pp. 173-174.

[40]Ibid., p. 149. Letter 4, Abelard to Heloise.

[41]Muckle, Adversities, Hist. Cal., p. 36.

[42]Ibid., p. 36. From his footnote.

[43]Ibid., Hist. Cal., p. 37. [44]Ibid., p. 38.

[45]Ibid., p. 71. [46]Ibid., p. 40

[47]Abelard, The Letters of Abelard and Heloise,
trans. Radice, p. 117. Letter 1, Heloise to Abelard.

[48]Ibid., p. 285. Letter 167, Heloise to Peter
the Venerable. There is mention of an Astralabe
on record as a canon of the Cathedral of Nantes in
1150, and as Abbot of a Cistercian abbey at Haute-
rive in the Swiss canton of Fribourg. Heloise re-
quested that Peter the Venerable help find a prebend for her son in November 1143, and he replied
that he would do his best.

[49]Ibid., Hist. Cal., p. 77.

[50]Muckle, Adversities, Hist. Cal., p. 41.

[51]Abelard, The Letters of Abelard and Heloise,
trans. Radice, p. 77. Betty Radice suggests that
Abelard had a sincere conversion once he had
entered the monastery at St. Denis and was an up-
holder of faith and the monastic rule like St.
Bernard, but in his own way. Ibid., p. 20.

[52]Muckle, Adversities, Hist. Cal., p. 43.

[53]Ibid. [54]Ibid., p. 46. [55]Ibid.

[56]John 7:25-26.

[57]Muckle, Adversities, Hist. Cal., p. 45.

[58]Ibid., p. 49. [59]Ibid., p. 53.

[60]Ibid., p. 55. [61]Ibid., p. 56.

[62]Abelard, The Letters of Abelard and Heloise,
trans. Radice, Hist. Cal., p. 90.

[63]Muckle, Adversities, Hist. Cal., p. 61.

[64]Ibid., p. 60. [65]Ibid., p. 63.

66Ibid., p. 63, n.1.   67Ibid., p. 63.

68Ibid., p. 64.

69David E. Luscombe, The School of Peter Abe-
lard. The Influence of Abelard's Thought in the
Early Scholastic Period (Cambridge: University
Press, 1969), p. 52.

70Muckle, Adversities, Hist. Cal., p. 65.

71Ibid., p. 66.   72Ibid., p. 69.   73Ibid.

74Ibid., p. 75.

75Abelard, The Letters of Abelard and Heloise,
trans. Radice, p. 25.

76Muckle, Adversities, Hist. Cal., p. 70.

77Ibid.   78Ibid., p. 77.

79Sikes, Peter Abailard, p. 235.

80Abelard, The Letters of Abelard and Heloise,
trans. Radice, p. 275. Letter 98, Peter the Venerable to Pope Innocent II.

81McCabe, Peter Abelard, p. 363, from the
Apologia.

82Abelard, The Letters of Abelard and Heloise,
trans. Radice, p. 270, from Abelard's "Confession
of Faith."

83Sikes, Peter Abailard, p. 237.

84Abelard, The Letters of Abelard and Heloise,
trans. Radice, p. 282. Letter 115, from Peter the
Venerable to Heloise.

85Sikes, Peter Abailard, p. 237.

CHAPTER TWO

ABELARD AS AN EDUCATOR, PHILOSOPHER,

AND THEOLOGIAN

In order to ascertain the impact Peter Abelard had on Medieval thought, it is necessary to investigate his role as an educator, philosopher, and theologian, for his doctrines stirred two councils to condemn him and inspired Bernard, the mystic saint, to an uncharacteristically vehement denunciation. Abelard's first studies were in philosophy, but after his parents entered the religious life and he had bid his mother farewell, Abelard turned his attention to theology. It was after this transition--during which time he attempted to apply the rules and logic of philosophy to theology--that Abelard began to run counter to the ecclesiastical current and found himself subject to public censure.

Abelard's own educational background was characterized by conflicts with his masters. In order to trace the influences in his teaching, it is necessary to review the viewpoints of his masters and scholarly roots of his studies. He studied under Roscelin (c. 1050-1120), William of Champeaux (c. 1070-1121), and Anselm of Laon (1040-1117), and read works by Boethius (c. 480-524), Aristotle (383-322 B.C.), Porphyry (c. 200's A.D.), and John Scotus Erigena (c. 800-850), whose De devisione naturae was condemned by Pope Honorius III at the Council of Sens, January 25, 1125, because of its possible pantheistic interpretation.

The logical works of Aristotle known in

Abelard's time were the <u>Categories</u>, <u>de Interpreta-</u>
<u>tione</u>, and the <u>Analytics</u>. These were suppliment-
ed by Porphyry's <u>Isagoge</u> (an introduction to
Aristotle's <u>Categories</u>), and by Boethius' <u>Commen-</u>
<u>taries</u>. Boethius translated the <u>Isagoge</u> and also
Aristotle's <u>Topics</u>, and probably his <u>Sophistical</u>
<u>Arguments</u>, along with the previously stated works
of Aristotle.[1] He also commented upon Cicero's
works: <u>Introductio ad categoricos syllogismos</u>
(<u>Introduction to the Categories of Syllogisms</u>),
<u>De Categoricis syllogismis</u> (<u>On the Categories of</u>
<u>Syllogisms</u>), <u>De hypotheticis</u> (<u>On Hypothesis</u>), <u>De</u>
<u>divisione</u> (<u>On Divisions</u>), and <u>De topicis differ-</u>
<u>entis</u> (<u>On Different Topics</u>).[2]

Abelard's first master was Roscelin, who was
born at Compiègne and studied at Soissons and
Paris. Roscelin is generally regarded as the
first nominalist; his only surviving writing is a
letter he wrote to Abelard on the Trinity. His
ideas are known through references made by other
writers such as Abelard and Anselm,[3] and it is
known that in 1092 he was condemned by the Council of Soissons because by refusing to recognize
the reality of universals he had strayed into the
heresy of Tritheism. Roscelin defined universals
as mere sounds, in which the individual became
the total expression of reality which could be
neither divisible in itself nor a part of a whole.
This led to three separate Gods rather than a
unity of the divine Persons.[4] In his attempt to
preserve dogma, Roscelin added that while the
three divine Persons were independent beings, they
had only one will and one and the same power.
Abelard refuted this extreme viewpoint in his own
teaching, just as he rejected the opposite opinion held by William of Champeaux.

William had studied under Manegold, Anselm
of Laon, and Roscelin, and his views on universals are primarily known through Abelard's <u>His-</u>
<u>toria Calamitatum</u>. William believed that the
species existed fully in every individual, which
was in turn differentiated by local modifications
or accidents. Thus, while maintaining the unity

38

of the species, he sacrificed the individual and was successfully challenged on this point by Abelard. William then modified his stance to one of non-difference--two individuals were united in the same species by an absence of differences.[5] Although Abelard also attacked this change, it affected his later views nevertheless. William had also used the attributes of power, wisdom, and love or goodness to describe the divine Persons of the Trinity,[6] and this figured in Abelard's later writings on the Trinity. William's theories on original sin being present in children as the spiritual sin of Adam was a stepping stone for Abelard's proposition on the importance of intention in sin. Already William had softened St. Augustine's view of men being born as sinners and Abelard carried the theory further.

Abelard's studies under Anselm of Laon also helped to shape his career. Anselm's school was characterized by an extreme fidelity to the scriptures and Church authorities. Anselm's school gave the impetus to the scholastic method of systematic arrangement of theological sentences, and Abelard's popular Sic et Non spread this system throughout the schools of France. Abelard, in contrast to the school of Laon, emphasized the love and example Christ offered to merit as an essential aspect of the Incarnation. Abelard, as a result, influenced Anselm's followers in the area of moral discussions, and the antagonisms between Abelard and Anselm's followers partly provoked his second trial for heresy.

Abelard's writings enjoyed great renown, and Bernard of Clairvaux complained in his letter to Pope Innocent II that "His writings have passed from country to country, and from one kingdom to another."[7] But Abelard was also an outstanding representative of the peripatetics, or wandering scholars who gathered a following of students as they traveled. He mentions in his Historia Calamitatum the flocks of students who gathered to hear him, "a famed and learned master admired by all,"[8] at Mount Ste. Geneviève and at the

Paraclete, although Master Hilary refered to the latter gathering as a disorderly mob.

It was Abelard's innovative instruction as well as his mental agility which brought students to him. His emphasis on the rational process led to a change in teaching methodology wherein the style of reading and meditation on texts gave way to disputation and discussion. A problem would be presented as a question and after the arguments both for and against it were stated, a balance was found. The traditional method of commenting upon a text with glosses was replaced by the Socratic method of an exchange of opinion between the master and his student. Abelard's method as demonstrated in his <u>Sic et Non</u> led to the use of the systematic framework of a formula utilizing definitions, distinctions, objections, arguments pro and contra, and syllogistic reasoning to arrive at a solution which appeared in later scholastic sentences and summae. Abelard encouraged his students to question matters, provided the Church had not already passed judgment on them. Otherwise,

> . . . the reader or auditor is free to
> judge, so that he may approve what is
> pleasing and reject what gives offense,
> unless the matter is established by
> certain reason or by canonical authori-
> ty . . . This questioning excites
> young readers to the maximum effort
> in inquiring into the truth, and
> such inquiry sharpens their minds.
> Assiduous and frequent questioning is
> . . . the first key to wisdom.[9]

When the scholastic method was applied to theology, it brought the use of philosophy into the study of theological questions. The doctrines became formally arranged and the systemization of theories constituted a rationalization of universal questions.

Not only did Abelard's new method of teaching

prove an attraction for students, but his elo-
quence in speech and his lucidity in criticism and
exposition also served to draw them to his school.
His student, John of Salisbury, wrote in his Metalogicon that Abelard

> . . . prefered to instruct his disciples
> and expedite their progress by more ele-
> mentary explanations, rather than to
> lose them by diving too deep into . . .
> (a) question.[10]

Abelard's concern for precise speech is evident
in his Sic et Non where he states that:

> Our . . . full understanding is impeded
> especially by unusual modes of expres-
> sions and by the different significances
> that can be attached to one and the same
> word . . . Just as there are many
> meanings so there are many words . . .
> so it is appropriate to use a variety
> of words in discussing the same thing.[11]

Abelard called philosophy the science of dis-
cernment and divided it into physics, ethics, and
logic; logic predominated. His superior skill in
the use of logic--for his distinctive manner centered around his persistent criticism of the
meaning of words and their proper useage--caused
Abelard to hold his less capable seniors and
former masters in a low regard. At the same time,
John of Salisbury noted in the Metalogicon that
Abelard disapproved of figurative speech on the
basis that "it is not permissible to stretch
figures, which are themselves only accepted as a
matter of expedience."[12] The questioning attitude of his students pleased Abelard; he was liberal in accepting arguments, but he rarely agreed
to admit hypothetical propositions in a logical
discussion, "unless forced to do so by manifest
necessity."[13] John of Salisbury said that Abelard

> . . . restricted admissible hypothetical
> propositions exclusively to those whose

41

consequent is included in its antecedent, or whose antecedent is voided if
its consequence be disproved.[14]

Although Abelard dominated the twelfth century teaching scene, he was nevertheless described
by Jocelyn--the logician and later Bishop of
Soissons--as a "quibbling scoffer rather than a
disputant, a jester rather than a teacher."[15] St.
Bernard of Clairvaux, in his Contra Errores Abelardi, condemned Abelard's approach to sacred
learning and Abelard's principle, as expressed in
his Sic et Non, that "it is not presumptuous to
judge concerning those by whom the world itself
will be judged."[16] Bernard wrote of Abelard:

> . . . he has no feeling either of piety
> or allegiance to the faith . . . God
> forbid that Christian faith should
> have these limits! These ideas and
> opinions belong to the Academics, who
> doubt of all things and know nothing.[17]

Abelard expounded on his philosophical doctrines in three general textbooks of logic. The
earliest treatise, the Logica Ingredientibus, contains commentaries on Porphyry's Isagoge and
Aristotle's Categories and De Interpretatione.
His second text is the Nostorum petitioni Sociorum
and all that survives of this is a commentary on
Porphyry. Abelard's last philosophical work is
the Dialectica, which may well represent his de-
finitive doctrine, and is an original textbook of
logic.

By the twelfth century, logic had come to be
regarded by many as a science of words, primarily
because Boethius took the ten categories of Aristotle, as preserved by Porphyry, which classified
the particular attributes of a substance to mean
terms rather than things.[18] Abelard himself, in
his Logica Ingredientibus, borrowed from Boethius
in listing his three species of philosophy as:

> . . . speculative, which is concerned

with speculation on the nature of things,
moral, for the consideration of the
honorableness of life, rational, for com-
pounding the relation of arguments, which
the greeks call logic. However, some
writers separated logic from philosophy
. . . because obviously, the other parts
work in logic in a manner, when they use
its arguments to prove their own questions.[19]

But Abelard differed from Boethius in that Abelard
was a dialectician who was essentially interested
in a critical approach to the meaning of words
and concepts. He continued to say in his Logica
Ingredientibus that

. . . he who will write logic perfectly,
must first write of simple words, then of
propositions, and finally devote the end
of logic to argumentation, just as our
prince Aristotle did, who wrote the
Categories on the science of words, the
On Interpretation on the science of propositions, the Topics and the Analytics
on the science of argumentations.[20]

It was through Abelard's influence that logic and
grammar, which had been declining in importance,
became drawn to dialectic where Abelard taught
concern for the words rather than writing style.
He noted in the Ingredientibus that

. . . the ambiguous treatment of logic
as well as grammar leads many, who do
not distinguish clearly the property of
the imposition of nouns or the abuse of
transference, into error by the transference of nouns.[21]

Early in his career, Abelard was caught up in
the philosophic controversy over the reality of
universals centered around the three questions
raised by Porphyry and left unanswered in his Isagoge. The first asked whether or not universals

43

were real or mere verbal expressions. The second
question asked if the universals were real, were
they corporeal (possessing form) or incorporeal
(without substance). The third question asked
whether or not universals existed separately or
were to be found in sensible things. Abelard's
innovation as stated in the Ingredientibus was to
introduce a fourth question:

> . . . whether genera and species must
> have something subject to them by nom-
> ination, or whether, if the things
> named were destroyed, the universal
> could still consist of the meaning only
> of the conception, as this noun rose
> when there is not a single rose to which
> it is common.[22]

John of Salisbury summarized the conflicting
viewpoints in his Metalogicon in 1159:

> One holds that universals are merely
> word sounds, although this opinion,
> along with its author, Roscelin, has
> already almost completely passed into
> oblivion. Another maintains that uni-
> versals are word concepts, and twists
> to support his thesis everything that
> he can remember to have ever been writ-
> ten on the subject. Our Peripatetic
> of Pallet, Abelard, was ensnared in this
> opinion. He left many, and still has,
> to this day, some followers and pro-
> ponents of his doctrine.[23]

Those who maintained that universals were merely
words were called nominalists. They believed that
only the individual existed and that the genus or
the species described by Aristotle had no connec-
tion to the real world. Those called realists
recognized the existence of genera and species and
their correspondence to reality.[24] Extreme
realists saw the individual as a mere variant of a
common essence, while moderate realists saw universals as separate entities which were nevertheless

44

present in individuals. This issue spanned the careers of Roscelin and Abelard, but it did not go beyond the contemplation of being and its relation to knowledge.

Boethius had considered the individual as the embodiment of the universal with only accidents making differences, and Roscelin considered the individual to be real while the universal was a mere word. Abelard rejected both concepts saying that realism denied the individual its own essence, and nominalism denied the evidence of reality. Abelard used his glosses on Porphyry to instruct his reader in the five subjects of Aristotle's <u>Categories</u> (genus, species, difference, property, and accident) in order to apply the lessons to logically explain the nature of universals and answer the four questions.

Abelard's solution paved the way for the later acceptance of translations of Aristotelian and Arabian works in the thirteenth century, and thus foreshadowed the new impetus these works gave to metaphysics. Universals, then, became part of the wider problems of theology and metaphysics. Abelard attempted to produce a theory of abstraction based on particular images when he concluded that universals were generalized images[25] and mental words rather than mere vocal sounds.[26] Even so, Abelard retained the concept of Platonic Ideas: "Ideas exist as patterns of things in the divine mind."[27]

To answer the questions of universals, Abelard said in the <u>Ingredientibus</u> firstly that concepts exist only in the intellect but signify real things, confusedly and indistinctly.

> . . . they signify by nomination things
> truely existent . . . and in no wise are
> they located in empty opinion; neverthe-
> less they consist in a certain sense in
> the understanding alone and naked and
> pure.[28]

He then stated that universals were corporeal and sensible insofar as they are words, but incorporeal in signifyin many similar individuals.

> . . . the universal names themselves are
> called both corporeal with respect to
> the nature of things and incorporeal with
> respect to the manner of signification,
> because although they name things which
> are discrete, nevertheless they do not
> name them discretely and determinately.[29]

The third question was answered by finding both Aristotle and Plato correct. Universals exist in sensible things when signifying the form of sensible things, and also independently of the sensible world, as in abstract conceptions.

> . . . they signify both sensible things
> and at the same time that common con-
> ception which Priscian ascribes particu-
> larly to the divine mind.[30]

And in answering his own fourth question, Abelard stated that if the individual ceased to exist, the universal would retain its meaning in the intellect.

> . . . we in no wise hold that universal
> nouns are, when, their things having been
> destroyed, they are not predicable of
> many things inasmuch as they are not
> common to any things, as for example the
> name of the rose when there are no longer
> roses, but it would still, nevertheless,
> be significative by the understanding,
> although it would lack nomination; other-
> wise there would not be the proposition:
> there is no rose.[31]

Abelard's treatment of universals gave rise to two important scholastic theses. He distinguished between the nature of sensible and imaginative perception and abstract perception, and he concluded that it is from the information provided by the senses that abstract perception draws its content, much in the way that colors deliniate the design in a picture.[32]   The universal concepts are formed by abstraction through concentrating attention on one aspect of a thing and disregarding its other aspects.   One first grasps an object without distinguishing its parts or properties, until with understanding, greater attention is focused on the object and it is grasped more distinctly as its properties are analyzed.[33]

The main authorities used by Abelard in logic were Aristotle's <u>Organon</u>, which is comprised of the <u>Prior Analytics</u>, the <u>Topics</u>, and the <u>Sophistical Questions</u>, and the works of Boethius.   To these sources, in the area of grammar, he added Priscian and Donatus and, in rhetoric, he added Cicero and Martianus Capella.[34]   Nevertheless, Abelard was not as well-versed in Aristotle and the sciences as were his contemporaries in the school of Chartres,[35] perhaps because his restless and energetic mind precluded the patience necessary to thoroughly study under a master for any length of time.   Possibly, if he had been able to discipline himself into following a stricter educational program he would have begun with a more solid base and could have gone further in his philosophy than he did.   Instead, his doctrines were determined by the masters he had studied under in the scope of conflict and refutation.   With a more thorough background, Abelard might have been able to shake free of their mistakes and presumptions to explore new philosophical territory on his own.   Abelard was condemned not because his ideas were in themselves controversial, but because his legion of followers tried to continue from where he had left off, and they for the most part were unable to master, as Abelard had, the subtleties of distinctions by which they could avoid accusations of paganism.

The <u>Dialectica</u> of Peter Abelard, written as a text about 1121-1125,[36] forms an independent work on logic in which the parts of speech and the

47

categories of thought are rationally analyzed since, for Abelard, logic and dialectic were used to distinguish valid arguments from fallacious ones. The _Dialectica_ was dedicated to Abelard's brother, Dagobert, possibly in response to his request for material for the instruction of his sons (and perhaps also Astralabe). Of the five treatises of this work, the first is missing but is referred to elsewhere in the _Dialectica_, and the ending treatise is incomplete. Since the manuscript was located at the Priory of St. Victor--which had been founded in 1108 by William of Champeaux--these parts may have been suppressed if they contained a sharp attack on the founder.[37]

The _Dialectica_ began with a treatment of the parts of speech in the first treatise and included an exposition of the Aristotelian _Categories_ as presented by Boethius and a discussion on the _dictiones_ (dictions), a group of significative terms. The tract ended with a commentary on the first three chapters of Aristotle's _De Interpretatione_.[38]

The second treatise centered on propositions and syllogisms, affirmation and negation, Fate and Providence, and ended with a commentary on Aristotle's _De Interpretatione_ and Boethius' _De Syllogismis categoricies (On Categories of Syllogisms)_.[39] The third tract covered topics according to Abelard's own divisions.[40] The fourth treatise dealt with hypothetical propositions and included a defense against his opponents' criticisms. It concluded with a paraphrase of the _De syllogismis hypotheticis (On Hypothetical Syllogisms)_ of Boethius.[41] Divisions and difinitions were covered in the fifth treatise and ended with a paraphrase of Boethius' _De divisionible et diffinitionibus (On Divisions and Definitions)_.[42]

But Abelard intended the _Dialectica_ to be more than merely a commentary on Porphyry, Aristotle, and Boethius. Instead, he presented a theory of Truth in this work which contained many of the same elements that would be found in the speculations on truth and falsity in the thirteenth and fourteenth centuries.[43] Abelard believed that sound understanding of dialectic would provide one with the weapons needed to defend the faith against the heresies of false philosophers. Thus, in the _Dialectica_, Abelard began to apply the elements of dialectic to form a harmony between faith, authority (dogma), and reason.[44] It was when some of the elements were considered apart from the whole that Abelard was accused of espousing various heresies.[45] But Abelard was careful to call reason an aid to faith. In the event of a conflict between the two, faith rather than reason was to prevail. In this respect, Abelard was not so much a rationalist as a Christian philosopher, but he planted the seeds for the later development of rationalism.

In applying the dialectic approach to understanding the problems of faith, Abelard took care to avoid accusations of heresy, but the rift between his admirers and his critics was firmly established and the extreme cry of heresy was inevitable. Abelard's work in theology centered on the themes of God's existence, the Trinity, the Incarnation, grace, and Christian morality or ethics, with regard to sin. Again, it was not so much his own errors in judgment which urged Bernard of Clairvaux and others to seek his condemnation, but Abelard's influence upon the minds of his students who attempted to carry on his work or formulate their own concepts based upon his theories. Indeed, the condemnation issued by Pope Innocent II on July 21, 1140 was directed not only against Peter Abelard, but also against his followers and supporters.[46] Abelard indirectly acknowledged the true cause of his condemnation when he wrote in his _Apologia_ about Bernard's criticism of his works:

> But you are so far from both my words
> and my meaning and you labour over argu-
> ments taken from your inventions rather
> than from my sayings . . . My friend
> has concluded his list of errors with

the remark: 'They are found partly in
his <u>Sentences</u>, and partly in his <u>Scito
te Ipsum</u>.' But I have never written a
book of <u>Sentences</u>, and therefore the remark is due to the same malice or ignorance as the errors themselves.[47]

Undoubtedly, he knew full well that the misquotes
had come from works written by his students.

Abelard did not try to relate his logical
discussions to a general theological outlook, but
distinguished between universals on the one hand
and divine ideas on the other. "Divine Ideas are
the archetypes that God has, as creator, while
man's ideas are quite different."[48] Abelard
claimed that he was content to leave matters of
dogma alone and to rely on the known authorities
while calling heresies poorly conceived dialectic.
He felt that he would be able to safeguard the
superiority of faith over the instrumental function
of reason in his theoretical relations and thus
escape heretical conclusions. In his <u>Theologia
Christiana</u>, Abelard wrote:

> . . . it should be a clear matter of
> reason that God far exceeds what can
> come under human discussion or the
> powers of human intelligence. Hence
> he cannot be seized upon in any par-
> ticular place or be comprehended by
> the human mind. It would be a great
> slight to the faithful if God pro-
> claimed Himself as accessible to petty
> human arguments or as definable in
> mere mortal words.[49]

Abelard characteristically exempted himself from
this category of dialecticians, but Bernard did
not. After Sens, he wrote of Abelard in a letter
to Cardinal Priest, Guy of Castello:

> When he speaks of the Trinity, he
> savours of Arius; when of grace, he
> savours of Pelagius; when of the

person of Christ, he savours of Nes-
torius.[50]

Peter Abelard defended his use of dialectics
and reasoning as the buttress for the foundation
of authority in his Introductio ad Theologian.
He stated that he did not intend to attack, con-
tradict, or replace traditional Church doctrines;
but Abelard nevertheless was accused of saying
that any faith which was not buttressed by reason
was merely an opinion or supposition. It could
be said that Abelard's precautionary admonishments
were an obvious and shallow attempt to placate his
would-be adversaries and that his effort was
doomed to failure as soon as his true intention
became known. He began his explanation of the
role of logic in Church doctrines in this way:

> To believe its doctrines is necessary
> for salvation. To understand them is
> not necessary . . . God's acts are not
> subject to the laws of science, and
> God's nature is not subject to the laws
> of logic . . . Authority is preferable
> to human reason in all matters, and
> . . . we rely on authority more safely
> than on human judgement.[51]

But then Abelard revealed his purpose more clearly as he went on to say that:

> The weapons with which faith is defended
> against psuedo-philosophy and psuedo-
> dialectic are true philosophy and true
> dialectic . . . We are obliged to en-
> deavor to understand rationally the
> doctrines which we believe, and especi-
> ally the fundamental doctrine of the
> Trinity.[52]

With his verbal skills, Abelard then deftly defended his position:

> Logic is the study of Logos; philosophy
> is the love of Sophia; Christianity is

the religion of Christ. Since Christ
is the true Sophia and Logos, to be a
Christian, to be a philosopher, and to
be a logician are synonymous phrases.[53]

Faith, charity, and sacraments were the three
main ideas forming the core to Abelard's other
ideas as expressed in his three general treatises
on theology.[54] These works, De unitate et Trinitate divina (condemned at Soissons in 1121), Theologia Christiana, and Introductio ad Theologian,
are similar in doctrine and even in wording, and
can be viewed as consecutive editions rather than
as three separate books.[55] The integral theme of
these books is an explanation of the doctrine of
the Trinity, which is most fully given in the
Theologia Christiana.

In addition to these works, Abelard produced
a collection of 156 theological questions, vari-
ously supported and opposed by authorities, in
order to work out a suitable solution by applying
the rules of logic. This work, Sic et Non, was
the first attempt at explaining theology from a
scientific rather than a meditational viewpoint.[56]
Abelard stated the basis for his method in the Prologue of his Sic et Non, when he wrote:

> . . . by doubting we come to inquiry;
> through inquiring we perceive the
> truth . . . [57]

Abelard's Scito te Ipsum contained his moral theology and concentrated on the problems of sin, enabling graces, and the powers of binding and
loosing granted to the bishops.

Abelard's concept ot God was different from
Roscelin's tritheism; God was not totally inacces-
sible to human reason:

> . . . the evidence given by nature for
> its creator and ruler makes God's exis-
> tence sufficiently obvious to any rea-
> sonable man . . . As to the Trinity, we

52

can show that, when considered rationally, it is the most plausible doctrine.
This is all that is necessary since we
are not teaching the faith by reason
but merely defending it.[58]

Prior to a revision of some of his opinions
on the Trinity, following the Council of Soissons,
Abelard depicted the unity of the Divine Persons
as expressions of power, wisdom, and benignity.
Wisdom was seen as a part of power, but benignity
was not a part of omnipotence.[59] Later, Abelard
changed his views so that the

Father was omnipotent, since He derives
His existence from Himself, and the
Spirit, not begotten, proceeded from the
eternally benign and the temporal in relation to creation only.[60]

In the Theologia Christiana, Abelard clari-
fied his points by defining the Trinity as having
the

. . . three necessary and sufficient
conditions of the highest good. It
must be perfectly powerful, perfectly
wise, and perfectly benevolent . . .
It is obvious, therefore, that the
highest good, which we call God, is a
trinity, since it consists in three
persons, God omnipotent, God omniscient,
and God omnibenevolent - all three
being one identical God.[61]

He redefined his terms to avoid accusations of
tritheism and meticulously explained his theory of
the Trinity as same in number and essence but not
in definition and property:

They are the same in number because there
is only one God . . . they are the same
in essence because, God having no parts,
whatever is God must be all of God . . .
They are different in definition because

53

> . . . God has numberless attributes
> . . . They are different in property
> (or prediction) because of the incom-
> patible properties of omnipotence,
> and omnibenevolence . . . each parti-
> cipate in all the divine attributes
> . . . But they do not participate in
> each other . . . which implies no
> difference in essence . . . [62]

Abelard retained his original premise of God as the
expression of power, wisdom, and benignity, but he
explained that God's omnipotence was compatible
with the determinism of His action, His omnisci-
ence was compatible with the free choice of crea-
tures, and His omnibenevolence was compatible with
the existence of evil.[63] Abelard altered his presentation after Soissons, but was still accused of
saying that there were three Gods. His subtleties
only served to confuse his opponents and convince
them of the danger of his theories if taken to
logical extremes by his followers. He proposed a
limitation on God which was unacceptable in spite
of the reasonableness of it.

In his treatment of the Trinity, Abelard proposed that God could not prevent an evil event because by virtue of His reason, He determined every
happening and knew why evil ought to occur.[64]

> God is able to do whatever he wills and
> . . . nothing can resist his will . . .
> Since he could not possibly will other
> than he actually does will, it follows
> from the very fact of his omnipotence
> that he could not possibly do other than
> he actually does do.[65]

The evil that happened did so not because God
willed it, but because He did not will it not to
happen:

> . . . what he counsels well may be re-
> jected by the sinful free creature, and
> the consequent evil is permitted,

although not willed, by God.[66]

Men were saved because their nature could be
changed to accept God's counsel. God could not
save anyone since His will was unchangeable;
therefore, men had to change to accept God's will.

With his admiration for the classical philosophers, Abelard found it an easy matter to recon-
cile Plato and Aristotle to Christianity. He
believed that the pagan philosophers had perceived
the Trinity before Christ, and in the Theologia
Christiana, Abelard expressed his theory of salvation for those pagans who had lived holy lives and
had received a revelation from God.[67]

> Turning to the pagan philosophers, we
> find that they have taught the Trinity
> ever since Hermes, the most ancient
> philosopher we know . . . the Platonists
> . . . call the Father 'the Good,' the
> Son 'the Mind,' and the Holy Ghost 'the
> World Soul' . . . (which) means the cos-
> mic soul by which our souls are animated
> spiritually . . . the nature of divini-
> ty itself, actually has been, and so
> still can be, arrived at by reason
> alone.[68]

Abelard incited further controversy by his
interpretation on the meaning and purpose of the
Atonement. In his day, the Ransom Theory of the
Atonement prevailed in which men were considered
to be justly the property of Satan because of their
sinfulness. In his Expositio in Epistulam ad
Romanos (Commentary Upon St. Paul's Epistle to the
Romans), Abelard concluded that the Ransom Theory
presented God as less than perfect and unjust towards His Son. Indeed, God seemed to work with the
devil.[69] He then proposed an alternative wherein
the Atonement was not a vicarious punishment to
men, but a sacrifice demanded by God to satisfy
His outraged justice and borne by Christ to demonstrate the love of God.[70] Men are lead to abstain
from sin by the meaning of Christ's example and

love.

The Council of Sens (1140) condemned Abelard's
repudiation of the Ransom Theory of the Atonement
although Abelard had not denied that Christ also
liberated men from servitude to the devil. In
spite of Abelard's condemnation at Sens, however,
the Ransom Theory soon vanished from Catholic
theology.[71]

The propositions stated in the Scito te Ipsum
earned Abelard a place as one of the principle
moralists of his time. He referred ethical problems to the subjective conscience and made intention more important than a sinful act. An error
in judgment was sufficient to lessen the fault of
a sin. Sin only occurred when there was consent
to sin, that being a contempt offered to God by
the mind.[72] In the Scito te Ipsum, Abelard wrote
that

> The time when we consent to what is un-
> lawful is in fact when we in no way draw
> back from its accomplishment and are in-
> wardly ready, if given the chance, to
> do it . . . this disposition incurs the
> fullness of guilt; the addition of the
> performance of the deed adds nothing to
> increase the sin.[73]

Abelard formulated theories on what was the
basis of good and evil acts as well as on what was
sin. He concluded that a mere desire or a disposi-
tion to evil was not sinful in itself. With

> . . . the will for evil and the doing of
> evil . . . to will and to fulfill the
> will are not the same, . . . to sin and
> to perform the sin are not the same.[74]

Abelard also stated that sin was not a weakness of
the mind.

> We consider morals to be vices or virtues
> of the mind which make us prone to bad or

good works . . . mental vice of this
kind is not . . . the same as sin nor is
sin the same as a bad action.[75]

He continued, in the _Scito te Ipsum_, to deny that
what was natural could be sinful. Pleasure was
natural and so could not be a sin nor increase the
sinfulness of an act:

> . . . no natural pleasure of the flesh
> should be imputed to sin nor should it
> be considered a fault for us to have
> pleasure in something in which when it
> has happened the feeling of pleasure is
> unavoidable.[76]

This one proposition may have been Abelard's attempt to rationalize the ignominy of his earlier
relationship with Heloise into a lesser evil.
Abelard went so far as to say that no act was good
or evil in itself, and sin was defined instead as
consent to evil and the intentional despising of
God and His laws. Abelard distinguished between:

> . . . the vice of the mind which makes
> us prone to sinning and then the sin
> itself which we fixed in consent to
> evil or contempt of God . . . [77]

Virtue became a mental habit "as a natural
quality"[78] gained by human effort which contrasted
with the prevailing concept of virtue being based
upon grace. Abelard's first book on ethics focused on understanding sin and distinguishing sin
from vice, which was defined as the opposite of
virtue. He admonished his readers to "Strive
. . . in resisting vices . . . lest they entice us
into wrongful consent."[79] Book Two of the _Scito
te Ipsum_ was intended to "teach to doing good."[80]
Virtue was seen as obedience to God, and Abelard
began Book Two by stating that knowing that God
would not test the faithful beyond their ability
to withstand adversity made them more humble and
thankful. The faithful, then, "cannot be aliena-
ted from God's love."[81]

57

Abelard distinguished between venial sin, an "unwitting offense or slip, however grave . . ."[82] and mortal sin, a "deliberate offense against conscience, however small in itself . . . meriting damnation."[83] Original sin was a punishment rather than a fault in men according to Abelard, and this ran counter to St. Augustine and Catholic tradition. He stated that sin could not

> . . . be committed by little children who do not consent to evil or offer contempt to God; but the penalty for Adam's sin is incurred unless the sacraments intervene.[84]

Enabling graces were also rejected by Abelard, and free will was considered sufficient for goodness since free will was prepared by faith. There was no requirement for additional graces to be granted before each good act of the will.[85] Men would desire to do good because of God's promise of eternal beatitude. Reason and faith were combined as the means offered by God to teach men how to obtain God's grace and the method of achieving it.

Abelard borrowed from Origen in formulating his theories on the power of bishops to bind or loose the sins of men. This, too, caused concern among Abelard's critics for in his Scito te Ipsum he claimed that only those bishops who showed merit were granted this power as worthy successors of the apostles. Instead of actually binding or loosing, Abelard believed that bishops could only declare who was bound and who was loosed, for "sinners are first reconciled to God and then loosed by the priests."[86]

The innovations Abelard introduced into theological study stemmed from his attempts at making faith intelligible to reason, and so it was probably Abelard whom Bernard of Clairvaux referred to in his third Sermon for the Feast of Pentecost as men who:

. . . called themselves philosophers
. . . should rather be called the slaves
of curiosity and pride.[87]

There was an inevitable conflict between
Christian theology and pagan philosophy, but Abe-
lard considered the two as essentially the same.
He wrote in the Logica Ingredientibus that:

> Plato's knowledge of nature and the reve-
> lations vouchsafed him from God left
> only a few of the mysteries of Christi-
> anity beyond his grasp.[88]

This theme was further developed in the Theologia
Christiana and caused his enemies to accuse Abelard of being a pagan. Many of Abelard's pro-
nouncements were incorrect by traditional standards, and could have weakened the expression of
Christian truth if carried to their logical conclusions,[89] but Abelard was also of an argumenta-
tive nature, and it could well be that he was
taken by his temperament beyond his own inclination in his writings. In his "Confession of Faith,"
Abelard emphasized that he did not desire to be a
philosopher if it meant not being a Christian.[90]

In later centuries, Abelard came to be seen
as a necromancer, a companion of the devil, a se-
nile fool, and as one who introduced secular philosophy into the study of theology.[91] In his own
time, Abelard felt misunderstood. He claimed that
he had not taught anything heretical but that
others, especially St. Bernard, were not familiar
with dialectical subtleties. Instead of subvert-
ing faith with reason, Abelard thought that he was
aiding faith through understanding. His dialectic
method of question and solution, as used in the
Sic et Non, had been used by eleventh century
canonists like Bernold of Constance (died 1100)
and Ivo of Chartres (died 1116),[92] but Abelard's
innovation was to apply the method to doctrines of
faith rather than to law.

While the condemnations of Soissons and Sens

showed a mistrust of philosophy, Abelard's contribution marked a turning point in Medieval philosophy. His solution of the problem of universals caused exaggerated realism to decline and disappear.[93] It could also be argued that Abelard's theology lacked constructive power and spiritual insight, but his school was imitated by others who wrote summas and sentences.[94] Abelard recognized that he was not so much a teacher of truth as an analyst whose primary concern was revealing problems, reorganizing the vocabulary of thought, and pointing out exaggerated or ignored themes from scriptures and the Church Fathers.[95] The objective of Abelard could be stated as not the attaining of truth per se, but only probability concerning God.[96] The use of dialectic had been growing since the tenth century, but it was Abelard who brought it into the realm of theology as an orderly method of discussion and verification.[97]

Abelard's impact upon the twelfth and thirteenth century schools of thought was not a passing one for he had trained a number of masters and scholars who traveled to cities throughout Europe and carried on his work. His followers included theologians, logicians, grammarians, poets, and administrators who became important figures in promoting Abelardian scholasticism and forming a link with the other schools of France. In the Metalogicon, John of Salisbury acknowledged the contribution made by Abelard,

> . . . the Peripatetic from Pallet, who won such distinction in logic over all his contemporaries that it was thought that he alone really understood Aristotle . . . Thanks to the work and diligence of . . . (such) masters, the arts regained their own, and were reinstated in their pristine seat of honor.[98]

CHAPTER TWO FOOTNOTES

1Maurice De Wulf, <u>History of Mediaeval Phi-</u>
<u>losophy</u>, vol. 1: <u>From the Beginning to the End of</u>
<u>the Twelfth Century</u>, 6th ed., trans. Ernest C.
Messenger (New York: Dover Publications, Inc.,
1952), p. 58, n. 2. De Wulf cites B. Geyer's <u>Die</u>
<u>alten lat, Uebersetzungen d. aristotelischen An-</u>
<u>alytik, Topk, u. Elenchik</u>, in which Geyer indi-
cates that his research shows that Abelard had
read <u>Sophistical Arguments</u> and quotes the <u>Prior</u>
<u>Analytics</u> of Aristotle.

2Ibid., p. 108.

3Gordon Leff, <u>Medieval Thought. St. Augus-</u>
<u>tine to Ockham</u> (Baltimore: Penguin Books, 1958),
p. 105. Roscelin's teachings are also mentioned
by John of Salisbury, an anonymous epigrammist,
and the account of the <u>De generibus et speciebus</u>
of Abelard. The last source is mentioned by De
Wulf, p. 149 of the previously cited work.

4Ibid., p. 106. Since Roscelin defined universals as mere sounds, the individual became the
total reality, neither divisible in itself nor
part of a whole, and this made any theological application bound to end in heresy. Roscelin repudiated his doctrines in 1092 at Soissons, but returned to them later.

5Ibid.

6Luscombe, <u>The School of Peter Abelard</u>, p. 174,
n. 3. The attributes of power, wisdom, and love
were commonly given to the Trinity prior to Abelard but came to be considered indicative of his

teaching.

[7]St. Bernard of Clairvaux, The Letters of St. Bernard of Clairvaux, trans. Bruno Scott James (London: Burns, Oates and Washbourne, Ltd., 1953), p. 318. Letter 239, written after the Council of Sens in 1140.

[8]John of Salisbury, The Metalogicon. A Twelfth Century Defense of the Verbal and Logical Arts of the Trivium, trans. with an introduction and notes by Daniel D. McGarry (Berkeley: University of California Press, 1962), p. 95. Quoted from Book II, Chapter 10 of The Metalogicon wherein John of Salisbury described his brief studies with Abelard. "At his feet I learned the elementary principles of this art (dialectic and logic) . . ."

[9]Brian Tierney, The Middle Ages, vol. I, Sources of Medieval History, 2nd ed. (New York: Alfred A. Knopf Publisher, 1973), p. 147. This work contains the translation of Abelard's Introduction to the Sic et Non, and Abelard states that "the reader or auditor is free to judge," indicating the provocative nature of this book.

[10]John of Salisbury, Metalogicon, p. 146, from Book III, Chapter 1.

[11]Tierney, Sources of Medieval History, p. 146, from Sic et Non.

[12]John of Salisbury, Metalogicon, p. 149, from Book III, Chapter 1.

[13]Ibid., p. 177. Book III, Chapter 6.

[14]Ibid.

[15]Luscombe, The School of Peter Abelard, p. 10, from the Vita Gosvini, ed. Bouquet, Recueil, XIV, pp. 442-443.

[16]Tierney, Sources of Medieval History, p. 145,

from <u>Sic et Non</u>. Abelard went on to say that
since there are contradictory writings by the
"holy Fathers," either "our understanding is de-
fective" or the texts were incorrectly ascribed to
the saints or "Corrupted by the errors of scribes,"
p. 146. Yet he cited nothing from apocryphal
books or anything which a saint, such as Augustine,
later retracted and corrected, p. 147. Bernard's
tract was in the form of a letter to Pope Innocent
II.

[17]James Cotter Morison, <u>The Life and Times of
Saint Bernard, Abbot of Clairvaux A.D. 1091-1153</u>
(London: Macmillan and Company, 1877), pp. 317-
318. Bernard stated in this letter that Abelard
"defines faith as an opinion," but the term used
by Abelard is "existimatio," which may also be
translated as an appraisal, judgment, or estima-
tion.

[18]Leff, <u>Medieval Thought</u>, p. 105.

[19]Richard McKeon, ed. and trans., <u>Selections
From Medieval Philosophers</u>, vol. I, <u>Augustine to
Albert the Great</u> (New York: Charles Scribner's
Sons, 1929, renewal copyright 1957), p. 208.
McKeon presents the translated glosses on Porphyry,
from Abelard's <u>Logica Ingredientibus</u>.

[20]Ibid., p. 209, (Porphyry).

[21]Ibid., p. 255, (Porphyry). He went on to say
that Boethius "first throws it into confusion by
some sophistical questions and reasons, that he
may teach us later to free ourselves from them."

[22]Ibid., p. 219, (Porphyry).

[23]Herman Shapiro (ed.), <u>Medieval Philosophy.
Selected Readings From Augustine to Buridan</u> (The
Modern Library. New York: Random House, Inc.,
1964), p. 178. See Book II, Chapter 17 of <u>The
Metalogicon</u> of John of Salisbury.

[24]Leff, <u>Medieval Thought</u>, p. 104.

[25]Carré, Realists and Nominalists, p. 57.

[26]David Knowles, The Evolution of Medieval Thought (Baltimore: Helicon Press, 1962), p. 112.

[27]Carré, Realists and Nominalists, p. 61.

[28]McKeon, Selections from Medieval Philosophers, p. 250, (Porphyry).

[29]Ibid., p. 252, (Porphyry).

[30]Ibid., p. 254, (Porphyry).   [31]Ibid.

[32]De Wulf, History of Mediaeval Philosophy, p. 199.

[33]Étienne Gilson, ed. A History of Philosophy, vol. II, Medieval Philosophy by Armand Augustine Maurer (New York: Random House, 1962), p. 66. Further references to this book will be under Maurer's name.

[34]Leff, Medieval Thought, p. 118.

[35]McKeon, Selections from Medieval Philosophers, p. 203. The author goes into great detail about the philosophy of the school of Chartres, but this will be considered in another chapter.

[36]Petrus Abaelardus, Dialectica, ed. with an Introduction by L. M. DeRijk, 2nd ed. revised (Netherlands: Van Gorcum and Company, 1970), p. xxi. Victor Cousin places the date towards the end of Abelard's life, but other datings divide the work by the separate treatises: Treatise I prior to 1121, Treatises II-IV in 1122-1123, and Treatise V after 1134. See p. xxii for details on dating this work. This book is in Latin with an English Introduction.

[37]Ibid., p. xiv.   [38]Ibid., p. xxix.

[39]Ibid., p. xxxi.

[40]Ibid., p. xxxii. Abelard used this section to sum up the divisions according to Themistius and Cicero and draw a mutual correspondence of them.

[41]Ibid., p. xxxiii.   [42]Ibid., p. xxxiv.

[43]Ibid., p. lix. DeRijk added that "Abailard frequently argues that only that proposition is a proper contradiction of another, which removes the sense of an expression and denies not more and not less than the original one stated . . . He calls the proposition . . . not particular, nor universal nor universal negative, but 'proper negation of the universal.'" This again demonstrated his leaning toward nominalism rather than toward realism.

[44]Ibid., p. xciii.   [45]Ibid., p. xciv.

[46]Luscombe, The School of Peter Abelard, p. 7. There are some who believe this letter should be dated in 1141, but it appears 1140 is more likely since it came when Abelard first arrived at Cluny, and Peter the Venerable spoke of Abelard spending his last years (rather than months) at Cluny, dying there in April 1142.

[47]Ibid., p. 109 and also: Joseph McCabe, Peter Abelard (New York: G. P. Putnam's Sons, 1901), p. 363. Both Luscombe and McCabe quote a portion of the Apologia of Abelard, with McCabe stating that his portion is the conclusion of the quote. The two portions have been linked in this paper for a more lucid reading.

[48]Leff, Medieval Thought, p. 112. Abelard also did not search for a meeting point between Divine Ideas and man's ideas.

[49]Peter Abelard, Abelard's Christian Theology, trans. J. Ramsay McCallum (Oxford: B. H. Blackwell, 1948; reprint ed., Merrick, New York: Richwood Publishing Company, 1976), p. 68.

[50]St. Bernard of Clairvaux, _Letters_, p. 321, from Letter 240.

[51]George Bosworth Burch, _Early Medieval Philosophy_ (New York: King's Crown Press, Columbia University, 1951), p. 70. Burch combined portions of Abelard's _De unitate et Trinitate divina_, _Introductio ad Theologian_, and _Theologia Christiana_, and then quotes Abelard's works jointly. This is acceptable since all three works are related editions of the same exposition of Abelard's theories. The doctrines in the cited quote refered to Church doctrines.

[52]Ibid., pp. 70-71, quoting Abelard.

[53]Ibid., p. 71, quoting Abelard.

[54]De Wulf, _History of Mediaeval Philosophy_, p. 201. The author considers this a characteris-division of subject matter for Abelard.

[55]Burch, _Early Medieval Philosophy_, p. 69. From Burch's introduction to his combined translation of Abelard's three main theological treatises.

[56]Leff, _Medieval Thought_, p. 112. Leff calls the _Sic et Non_ a milestone on the road to the scholastic system of the thirteenth century.

[57]Tierney, _Sources of Medieval History_, p. 147, from Abelard's _Sic et Non_ introduction. Abelard cited as an example of the appropriateness of questioning, Jesus' questioning of the doctors when he was twelve years old, as recounted in Luke.

[58]Burch, _Early Medieval Philosophy_, p. 72, quoting Abelard from his combined writings.

[59]Luscombe, _The School of Peter Abelard_, p. 154.

[60]Ibid., p. 155.

61Burch, *Early Medieval Philosophy*, p. 73, from Abelard's *Theologia Christiana*.

62Ibid., p. 76, from Abelard's *Theologia Christiana* and *De unitate et Trinitate divina*.

63Ibid., p. 78. Abelard gave an analogy of the bronze seal which drew great criticism, and is mentioned by Luscombe and Leff but not presented by them. Other sources refer to this analogy as being a copper seal. The analogy is quoted in Chapter Three of this paper. Abelard considered the analogy "The most perfect . . . for confounding the pseudo-philosophers . . ."

64Luscombe, *The School of Peter Abelard*, p. 156.

65Burch, *Early Medieval Philosophy*, pp. 73-74, from Abelard's *De unitate et Trinitate divina* and *Theologia Christiana*. Abelard went on to say

> What God has foreseen necessarily happens, but this does not imply that what God has foreseen happens necessarily. A thing can happen otherwise than God has foreseen it would happen, but it cannot happen otherwise than he has foreseen could happen, and it does not happen otherwise than he has foreseen it would happen.

66Ibid., p. 74, from Abelard's theological works.

67Maurer, *Medieval Philosophy*, p. 69. Abelard went on to say that these philosophers enlightened the pagans about God's will and so brought moral goodness and salvation within their reach. The oracles of the Sybylls could be considered an example of pagan inspiration concerning the Trinity.

68Burch, *Early Medieval Philosophy*, p. 72, from Abelard's *Theologia Christiana*.

[69]Roger B. Lloyd, The Striken Lute. An Account of the Life of Peter Abelard (Port Washington, New York: Kennikat Press, 1932), p. 169. The author gives a thorough explanation of the Ransom Theory.

[70]Ibid., p. 172. Love becomes raised to the supreme good, and is shown to be complete through sacrifice.

[71]Ibid., p. 216. In conjunction with the Ransom Theory, Abelard also stated that souls were incapable of movement, and so excluded the idea of a local motion in the descent of Christ's soul into Hell. This came from Abelard's "Exposition on the Apostle's Creed," and was also condemned. According to Luscombe, The School of Peter Abelard, p. 148, later works by Abelard's students indicate that he had taught that the "incarnation of Christ is called a descent with respect to the humiliation, not to movement in space . . . the last coming of Christ is explained either as an unusual event upon the earth or also as a local and real coming of Christ from the Heavens the divine omnipresence (being) an omnipresence of power."

[72]Peter Abelard, Ethics, trans. with an introduction by David E. Luscombe (Oxford: The Clarendon Press, 1971), p. 5. This work is also known as the Scito te Ipsum. Abelard states that "this consent we properly call sin . . . For what is that consent unless it is contempt of God and an offense against him?"

[73]Ibid., p. 15. [74]Ibid., p. 33.

[75]Ibid., p. 3. Luscombe believes that at this point Abelard may think of vice as a natural or innate human characteristic.

[76]Ibid., p. 21. Abelard was criticized on this point by William of St. Thierry in his Thirteen Propositions on Abelard's errors. See Bernard of Clairvaux: Studies Presented to Dom Jean

Leclercq. Cistercian Studies Series No. 23, Kalamazoo, Michigan: Cistercian Publications, Inc.,
1973, p. 71, "That he says in concupiscense, delight, and ignorance no sin is commited, and
things of this sort are not sin, but nature."

[77]Ibid., p. 33.

[78]Ibid., p. xxv. This was seen as an introduction of pagan moral themes into Christian theology.

[79]Ibid., p. 5. Abelard wrote that people
should resist vices because "through this they
have the material for a struggle so that triumph-
ing over themselves through the virtue of temper-
ance they may obtain a crown."

[80]Ibid., p. 129, from Book II of Abelard's
Ethics.

[81]Ibid., p. 131. Book II is incomplete and
ends at this point.

[82]Luscombe, The School of Peter Abelard, p.
169.

[83]Ibid.

[84]Ibid., p. 151. Original sin was not a fault
but a debt of punishment.

[85]Ibid., p. 275. Leff (p. 133) points out
that this meant that there was no need for super-
natural aid in committing a good act, which trans-
formed morality into a personal matter. The cri-
teria changed from an objective one to a subjective one.

[86]Ibid., p. 152. Abelard stated in his Ethics
(p. 119): "Origen shows this power was not con-
ferred by the Lord on all bishops, but only on
those who imitate Peter . . . in the dignity of
his merits."

[87]Étienne Gilson, Reason and Revelation in the Middle Ages (New York: Charles Scribner's Sons, 1938), p. 12.

[88]McKeon, Selections from Medieval Philosophers, p. 207.

[89]Knowles, The Evolution of Medieval Thought, p. 124.

[90]Abelard, The Letters of Abelard and Heloise, trans. Radice, p. 270. From Abelard's Confession of Faith written in a letter to Heloise and preserved by his student Berengar of Poitiers.

[91]Luscombe, The School of Peter Abelard, p. 12.

[92]De Wulf, History of Mediaeval Philosophy, p. 201.

[93]Ibid., p. 204

[94]Ibid., p. 243. Abelard's followers included Master Hermanus, Roland Bandinelli (Pope Alexander III), Omnibene, and an anonymous writer in the library of St. Florian.

[95]Luscombe, The School of Peter Abelard, p. 309.

[96]Paul Vignaux, Philosophy in the Middle Ages, An Introduction, trans. by E. C. Hall (New York: Meridian Books, Inc., 1959), p. 59.

[97]Leff, Medieval Thought, p. 93. The codifiers of canon law, such as Burchard of Worms, Ivo of Chartres, and Gratian, had already been using the question form of disputation in legal matters.

[98]John of Salisbury, Metalogicon, pp. 21-22.

CHAPTER THREE

ABELARD AS SEEN BY HIS CONTEMPORARIES

Hostility to Abelard and his school of thought began with his teachers, William of Champeaux (d. 1121) and Anselm of Laon (d. 1117), but their displeasure was not of the type to do him injury, but served rather to increase Abelard's fame and renown. William's efforts to prevent Abelard from opening his first school were unsuccessful,[1] and when William later was able to remove Abelard from the chair of dialectics at the cathedral school of Paris in 1109, Abelard was not particularly concerned, but said that "there was nothing he could do against me personally."[2] Anselm of Laon was also an ineffectual opponent who merely forbade Abelard to lecture in his school.[3] While the beginning of a more forceful antagonism to Abelard and his teaching could be dated from his conflicts at Laon with Alberic of Rheims and Lotulph the Lombard,[4] this could be interpreted as little more than the rivalry of fellow students. Indeed, Otto of Freising (c. 1114-1158) wrote that as a student, Abelard was

> . . . so conceited and had such confidence in his own intellectual power that he would scarcely so demean himself as to descend from the heights of his own mind to listen to his teacher.[5]

Therefore, the reaction of two of Abelard's fellow students may have been based on pure exasperation. But after Abelard entered St. Denis, the momentum of opposition began to build against him and even

71

those enemies who had been relatively unimportant began to present a serious threat to him.

There are two important factors to consider when examining the origins of Abelard's change in fortune after entering St. Denis, for until this time, he was eminently successful. The first factor as stated by Abelard himself was that "it was . . . confusion springing from shame . . . which drove me to the refuge of monastic cloister,"[6] and not religious inclination. And the second factor was that the shock of his mutilation from Fulbert's barbaric revenge had shaken Abelard's outlook on life. His optimism and self-assured attitude disappeared, and while he recovered his confidence sufficiently to return to the excitement of the schools, he did so with a trepidation previously unknown to him. Abelard's personality and his circumstances both underwent a dramatic change which made him suddenly vulnerable to his adversaries. No longer a cleric but a monk--and a rebellious one at that--Abelard found himself in a subservient position wherein he was expected to be obedient to an abbot whom he considered an intellectual inferior. He was now subject to the rules of the Benedictine religious order and to strict ecclesiastical censure, and the possibility of a very real seclusion from the world must have impressed itself upon Abelard once he realized that his mutilation would not damage his teaching reputation. As the potential consequences of his rash act became clear to him, Abelard set about to gain relative freedom from the bounds of St. Denis, and eventually re-opened his school at the priory of St. Ayoul in Provins where he taught philosophy and theology. Otto, Bishop of Freising, briefly recorded that Abelard then

> from being a keen thinker . . . became keener, from being a learned man he became more learned, to such a degree that after some time he was released from obedience to his abbot, came forth in public, and again assumed the office of teacher.[7]

By the time Abelard's tract <u>De unitate et Trinitate divina</u> was composed (c. 1118-1121), he was already embroiled in controversy. As as monk, Abelard's teaching of secular philosophy seemed incompatible with his vocation, and as a teacher not properly schooled in the Sacred Science, he seemed equally unqualified to teach theology. It was after he had entered the religious life that Abelard's enemies found the means of venting their envy and frustration and, thus, Abelard's previously inconsequential foes from Anselm's school in Laon, Alberic and Lotulph--as heads of the school of Rheims[8]--led the way by leveling charges of Sabellian heresy[9] against Abelard. The difficulty with Abelard's writing on the Trinity, as explained by Otto of Freising, was that

> he minimized too much the three persons which Holy Church has up to the present time piously believed and faithfully taught to be not merely empty names but distinct entities and differentiated by their properties. The analogies he used were not good, for he said among other things: 'just as the same utterance is the major premise, the minor premise, and the conclusion, so the same being is Father, Son, and Holy Spirit . . . [10]

The charges made against Abelard's teachings culminated in the Council of Soissons in 1121, and the method of attack employed by "those excellent men and acknowledged masters,"[11] as Otto called Alberic and Lotulph, became characteristic of future actions.

Unable to deal with Abelard's intellect and fearful of his ability at disputation, his rivals first incited the crowds against him with false rumors before Abelard arrived in Soissons and gave him no chance for rebuttal.[12] Reading of the offensive tract during the council's regular meeting proved uneventful and the much-awaited condemnation was postponed until the final day. In the

interim, an impassioned scene had occurred when
Alberic, as a follower of Gilbert de la Porrée--
who held the opinion that "as substance generates
substance, so the Father generates himself"[13]--
managed to embarrass himself in front of his
friends while attempting to argue this point with
Abelard. Alberic's objection was narrowed to an
accusation that Abelard had not adhered to recognized authority in his viewpoints in the disputed
tract.

> . . . he remarked that . . . I denied
> that God had begotten Himself . . . so
> I looked up the passage which I knew
> but which he had failed to see . . . a
> sentence headed 'Augustine, On The
> Trinity, Book One.' 'Whoever supposes
> that God has the power to beget Him-
> self is in error . . . There is nothing
> whatsoever which can beget itself' . . .
> I was ready to prove to him that by
> his own words he had fallen into the
> heresy of supposing the Father to be
> His own Son.[14]

Alberic lost his temper, shouted a few threats,
and went away angry and frustrated.[15]

The legate of Pope Calixtus II, Conon, Bishop
of Praeneste, decided to have Abelard return to
St. Denis and have the case examined more thoroughly, but Alberic and his accomplices felt that
this would have the appearance of defeat for them
and so managed to convince the legate to reverse
his decision and to "condemn the book without an
inquiry, burn it immediately in the sight of all,
and condemn (Abelard) to perpetual confinement in
a different monastery."[16] Public outcry saved
Abelard from a future of virtual imprisonment. He
was returned to St. Denis where he again contrived
to regain his freedom from the monastic way of
life.

Alberic and Lotulph were motivated by a jealousy that was apparent to anyone involved with the

Council of Soissons and its action against Abelard.
Even the legate recognized this to be true, according to Abelard in his Historia Calamitatum,[17] and while a rival's envy may make him a merciless adversary, his opposition will be tainted in the public eye. There were many people who spoke out against Abelard either directly or indirectly, but not with the righteous enthusiasm and moral conviction that Bernard of Clairvaux would later demonstrate at Sens. Such general criticisms, which were continued even after Abelard's death, were not likely to be effective in mustering public support to silence the famous teacher or to discredit his teaching even though Abelard was considered by many to be unfit to teach theology due to his lack of formal training, and certainly not to teach it using the tools of philosophy.

St. Peter Damiani (1007-1072) had vigorously attacked dialectics, grammar, and natural reason in general when applied to theology.[18] Sometime between 1120 and 1125, Guibert, Abbot of Nogent (c. 1064-1125) dictated a commentary on Hosea in which he denounced those

> who presume to discuss and examine the
> dogmas of the church on which they had
> once been nourished, treating like some-
> thing new matters defined by God and
> the Fathers . . . We see this today
> with certain grammarians who blindly
> seek to shine in commenting not only on
> Holy Scripture but even on any given
> heavenly mystery.[19]

And Clarembald of Arras, in his Commentary on Boethius' De Trinitate, credited Abelard with having "a spirit of boastfulness and impiety,"[20] and in 1138-1139, William of St. Thierry (c. 1119-1148) published a tract, Disputatio Adversus Abelardum, to point out the theological errors of Abelard. This tract listed thirteen propositions which stated as Abelard's heresies:

> 1. That he defines faith as an opinion

of things that are not seen.

2.   That he calls improper in God the names of Father, and Son, and Holy Spirit, but this description is of the fullness of the highest good.

3.   That the Father is full power, the Son a certain power, the Holy Spirit no power.

4.   Concerning the Holy Spirit, that He is not out of the substance of the Father and the Son, as the Son is out of the substance of the Father.

5.   That the Holy Spirit is the world-soul.

6.   That from free choice, without assiting grace, we can will and do well.

7.   That Christ did not for this reason assume flesh and suffer, to liberate us from the law of the devil.

8.   That Christ, God and man, is not the third person in the Trinity.

9.   That in the sacrament of the altar the form of the prior substance remains in air.

10.   That he says diabolical suggestions are brought about in men by natural science.

11.   That from Adam we do not get the guilt of original sin, but the penalty.

12.   That there is no sin, except in consent to the sin and in contempt of God.

13.   That he says in concupiscence, delight, and ignorance no sin is committed; and things of this sort are not sin, but nature.[21]

Much of the criticism leveled at Abelard, such as that of Walter of Mortagne, disclosed a fear "of the unhappy results which might follow from any . . . application of the method of the logicians to the problems of theology."[22]

Also seeking Abelard's condemnation prior to Sens was Hugo Metellus, who asked Pope Innocent II to condemn both Abelard and his theology since the famous teacher was

> . . . a second Pha ton who had mounted
> the chariot of the true Sun as its
> driver - into the chariot, that is,
> of the four Gospels - in order to illum-
> inate the world; he had not, however,
> proceeded on the right course and had
> ruined the world by the fire of his
> own pride.[23]

Even thirty-six years after his death, Abelard's teaching was yet the subject of spirited
debate, as evidenced by the treatise written by
Walter of St. Victor's, Contra Quattuor Labyrin-
thos Franciae (1178), in which four minotaurs--
Peter Abelard, Peter Lombard, Peter of Poitiers,
and Gilbert de la Porrée--were described as pre-
paring the way for the destruction of theology in
France through the labyrinth of philosophy.[24]
Philosophy was commonly considered to be the enemy
of theology, and the compatibility between the
classics and Christianity was enthusiastically
denied.

Geoffrey of Clairvaux expressed his opinion
of Abelard in a segment of the Vita Prima Bernardi
and summarized the major difficulty between Abelard and his contemporaries in theology. They considered him to be an outsider who could, through
pride and misinterpretation, wreak havoc upon the
Christian faith. Geoffrey wrote:

> Peter Abelard was without any doubt a
> great master and he was most celebrated
> for his learning. But with as little
> doubt his teaching on the Catholic faith
> was not faithful to tradition - rather
> it was a 'faithless faith.' His works
> were circulating in no time, dissemin-
> ating profane novelties in word and
> sense, together with the gravest blas-
> phemies.[25]

When Abelard used an analogy of a bronze seal

to describe the relationship of the three Persons
of the Trinity in his <u>Theologia Christiana</u>, William of St. Thierry's objections signaled the beginning of a conscientious effort, bolstered by
religious fervor, to silence Abelard once and for
all. Abelard had compared the Trinity to

> . . . a bronze seal, in which its mater-
> ial, the bronze, its form, the royal im-
> age, and its act, sealing the wax, are
> related to each other exactly as the
> persons of the Trinity are.[26]

But William claimed that such an analogy was Arian.

> The seal is formed only out of a certain
> quantity of copper, and in the actual
> process of sealing, no material is used,
> and so, when applied to the Trinity, the
> analogy makes the Son a kind of power
> . . . while the Spirit represented by
> the act of sealing, is no power . . . [27]

An unknown abbot also used this criticism in
a tract against Abelard's analogy, <u>Disputatio
Anonymi Abbatis,</u> and it was later one of St. Bernard's arguments against Abelard's teaching.[28]
Walter of Mortagne added his voice to the rising
complaints and accused Abelard of making the
Father alone powerful.[29]

Bernard of Clairvaux was finally persuaded to
take action by William of St. Thierry. William
wrote to Bernard and to Geoffrey of Chartres concerning Abelard:

> God knows I am all confusion when you
> are silent, whose business it is to
> speak when common weal urges that some-
> thing be done. I am nothing among men,
> but you are lords and fathers among the
> people, so I will force you to speak!
> I can see the faith being corrupted all
> around me, with no one resisting the
> attack, no one saying a word against

it . . .

> It is not small points that are being
> brought into question, but faith in the
> Holy Trinity, the person of our Mediator,
> Jesus Christ, the Holy Spirit, God's
> grace, the sacrament of our Redemption
> . . . Peter Abelard writes everything
> anew, teaches everything as it was
> never taught before, and his works have
> crossed the waters and the mountains,
> and are to be found everywhere. His
> doctrines are proclaimed with honour,
> and defended openly; even in the Roman
> curia . . .[30]

William then admonished Bernard and Geoffrey to
act quickly to crush the evil before it became
"the canon of faith, and no one will be found to
fight it."[31] Interestingly enough, after achieving his goal, William said of Abelard, "And yet I
loved him."[32]

The episode of the Council of Sens in 1140
and the interaction of Abelard and Bernard of
Clairvaux demonstrated further that it was not
Abelard himself or his personal beliefs that were
under attack, but his influence on the minds of
his students--he was encouraging them to explore
novel ideas and to question the long-accepted ones.
It was not so much the subject matter but the
method that was bearing dangerous fruit.

Otto of Freising mentioned the contest between Abelard and Bernard in his work, The Deeds
of Frederick Barbarossa. He described Bernard as

> . . . both zealous in his devotion to
> the Christian religion and somewhat cred-
> ulous in consequence of a habitual
> mildness, so that he had an abhorrence of
> teachers who put their trust in worldly
> wisdom and clung too much to human argu-
> ment. If anything at variance with the
> Christian faith were told him concerning

79

anybody, he would readily give ear.[33]

But in the same year as the Council of Sens, Bernard wrote a tract in the form of a letter to Pope
Innocent II called <u>Contra Errores Abelardi</u>, in
which he argued against Abelard's view of the purpose of Christ's death on the cross and reempha-
sized its redemptive value. Abelard was accused
of calling the crucifiction merely a means of pro-
viding man with an example of "supreme humility,
charity, and self-sacrifice," while Bernard contended that Christ's death "actually destroys sin
in souls and communicates . . . a new life which
is totally super-natural and divine."[34] This
would cause a complete regeneration of the soul
and gives one the gifts of justice, charity, and
love.

     When Bernard received the aforementioned let-
ter from William of St. Thierry, his response was
predictable and was quoted by Geoffrey of Clairvaux in the <u>Vita Prima Bernardi</u>.

          I judge the step you took to be just and
          necessary. I have not read Abelard's
          book completely, but what I have read
          is sufficient to tell me that his doc-
          trine is wrong and dangerous . . . I
          think we should confer about it some-
          where, you and I . . . What you exhort
          me to do, God with His good Spirit will
          enable me to perform.[35]

     Apparently, Bernard met with Abelard "in se-
cret so that he might try to correct his errors
without humiliating him in public."[36] Abelard was
said to have been so impressed by Bernard's humble
and reasonable attitude that he "became contrite
to the point of promising to alter everything as
Bernard should see fit."[37] Geoffrey of Clairvaux's
account of this meeting seems shaded when compared
to a letter Abelard had written to Bernard earlier
after the saint had visited the Paraclete and
found fault with the innovation to the Lord's
Prayer which had been introduced to the nuns by

Abelard. He was at the time still Abbot of St.
Gildas when he wrote to Bernard:

> You Cistercians, indeed, are so vehement
> in your adherence to such a course, that
> you keep it and defend it against the
> practice of all the churches. You,
> forsooth, novel upstarts, and not a
> little proud of your novelty, have de-
> cided on celebrating the Holy Office in
> a way opposed to the ancient, universal,
> and long-continued custom whether of
> monks or clerks. And yet you do not ex-
> pect to be blamed if this novelty or
> singularity of yours differs from antiq-
> uity, so long as you consider it conson-
> ant with reason and the tenor of the
> Rule; neither do you care for the won-
> der and objections of others, provided
> you follow what you think are your rea-
> sons.[38]

Instead of being contrite, Abelard decided to
request a public debate with Bernard and so he
"applied for a hearing to the Bishop of Sens, in
whose church a great council was to be held."[39]
Bernard first declined, but then agreed "lest his
absence should lend strength to Abelard's cause."[40]

The actions of Bernard at the Council of Sens
have become a subject of debate with some saying
that he acted reasonably and with proper intent,
while others claim that he literally rigged the
hearing. Prior to the Council of Sens, St.
Bernard met with the council members and presented
a list of nineteen _capitula_ (propositions) in
which he stated as the heresies of Abelard:

> 1. That the Father is full power, the
> Son a certain power, the Holy Spirit no
> power.
> 2. That the Holy Spirit is not of the
> substance of the Father or the Son.
> 3. That the Holy Spirit is the world-
> soul.

81

4. That Christ did not assume flesh to
liberate us from the yoke of the devil.
5. That neither God and man, not this
person which Christ is, is the third
person in the Trinity.
6. That free choice by itself suffices
for something good.
7. That God can do or forego only those
things, or only in that manner, or at that
time, in which he does, not in another.
8. That we did not contract guilt from
Adam, but only the penalty.
9. That they did not sin, who, ignorant,
crucified Christ, and that whatever is
done through ignorance is not to be
ascribed to guilt.
10. That in Christ there had not been a
spirit of fear of the Lord.
11. That the power of binding and loosing
was given only to the apostles, and not
to their successors.
12. That on account of works neither
better nor worse is brought about.
13. That to the Father, who is not from
another, properly or specially belongs
omnipotence, not however wisdom and goodness.
14. That also chaste fear is excluded
from future life.
15. That the devil instigates suggestion
by the application of stones or herbs.
16. That the advent at the end of the
world can be attributed to the Father.
17. That God neither ought nor can prevent evil.
18. That the soul of Christ itself did
not descend to Hell, but only through its
power.
19. That neither the deed nor the will
nor the desire, nor the delight which
moves it, is a sin, nor ought we wish to
extinguish it.[41]

Geoffrey of Clairvaux, however, writing after
Bernard's death, recounted the matter as a simple

direct confrontation.

> Bernard offered the offending passages
> in Abelard's work to the assemby,
> giving him the option of disclaiming
> them as his opinions, or humbly cor-
> recting them, or answering (if he
> could) objections put to him from the
> accepted authority of the fathers.[42]

Abelard was described as unwilling to admit his
mistakes and incapable of resisting Bernard's arguments, for

> as he said afterwards to his friends
> . . . his mind was a blank at the
> time, his memory and all his wits
> having forsaken him.[43]

The Council of Sens condemned the errors in
Abelard's works and was considered a victory for
Bernard of Clairvaux. Abelard's followers, however, claimed that he had been tricked into be-
lieving that he was attending a debate, but that
he was instead put into the position of a defendant, as at Soissons. The same tactics used by
Bernard and presented by Geoffrey as pious and
humble were rejected at the council held against
Gilbert de la Porrée a few years later.

After Abelard left the Council of Sens to
appeal to Rome, Bernard sent letters to Pope Innocent II and some of the cardinals he knew, such as
Stephen of Praeneste, Guy of Castello--who later
became Pope Celestine II in 1143 and who had once
been a student under Abelard--and Ivo of St. Laur-
ence, whom he scolded because of the popularity of
Abelard's books in Rome.[44]

In his letter to Innocent II, Bernard warned
that:

> Peter Abelard strives to make vain the
> merit of the Christian faith, since he
> believes he can comprehend by human

reason all that is God: he mounts up
to the heaven, he goes down to the
depths; there is nothing that is hid
from him, whether in the depth of
hell or in the height above . . . [45]

Abelard was vigorously denounced both for his personality and for his writings. There was even a
possible reference of a conspiracy between Abelard
and his friend and former student, Arnold of Brescia. Bernard continued in his letter on Abelard:

> . . . The man is great in his own eyes,
> disputing concerning the faith against
> the faith, exercising himself in great
> matters and in things too high for him,
> a searcher of his own glory, a contriver
> of heresies . . . That book of his has
> risen and appeared to many. Finally
> now she sends out her boughs unto the
> sea and her shoots unto Rome . . . Ac-
> cordingly, because that man draws the
> multitude after him and has a people
> that believe in him, it is necessary
> that you treat this disease with a
> swift-acting remedy . . .[46]

And in Bernard's compilation of Abelard's errors
--which he sent to Innocent II--he cautioned the
pope that

> The time has come for you to acknowledge
> your primacy, to prove your zeal and to
> honour your ministry . . . confirm the
> faith that vacillates in the hearts of
> Christians, and punish those who cor-
> rupt the faith, by means of your author-
> ity.[47]

In August of 1140, the pope responded favor-
ably to Bernard's request, and the news caught up
with Abelard at Cluny where he had been invited to
rest by Peter the Venerable. The pope's reply, as
recounted by Otto of Freising, had been sent to
Archbishops Henry of Sens and Samson of Rheims, as

well as to the Abbot of Clairvaux, and he quoted
an edict of Valentinian II and Marcion issued in
452, and cited the heresies of others, like Arius.

> Let no cleric or soldier or man of any
> other condition attempt hereafter to
> discuss the Christian faith in public
> . . . And those who transgress this law
> shall be punished as though they had
> committed sacrilege. Therefore, if
> there shall be any cleric who dares to
> discuss religion in public, he shall
> be removed from the company of the
> clergy. Moreover, we grieve that, as
> we learn from an inspection of your
> letters, . . . because of the pernicious
> doctrine of Master P. Abelard, the her-
> esies of those whom we have mentioned
> and other perverse dogmas have begun to
> spring up in opposition to the Catholic
> faith . . . we . . . have condemned the
> articles sent us by Your Discretion and
> all the perverse teachings of Peter
> himself, by the authority of the holy
> canons, together with their author, and
> we have imposed perpetual silence upon
> him as a heretic.[48]

The conclusion of the pope's letter addressed the
threat that was so sharply felt by Abelard's opponents: that of his followers.

> We decree also that all followers and
> defenders of this error be sequestered
> from the company of the faithful and
> restrained by the bond of excommunica-
> tion.[49]

The letter ends: "Given at the Lateran on the
Twelfth day before the Kalends of August . . . "
with the addition of the year 1141 by the translator. This date is debatable and is more likely to
have been 1140, since after Peter the Venerable
arranged for peace between Bernard and Abelard,
there would have been little reason for the pope

to go ahead with the condemnation which he later retracted anyway. The year 1141 is used by some historians as a means of denying that there was undue haste in the matter, but considering the later reversals this date does not appear justifiable. There was, indeed, undue haste followed by retractions which show that Abelard was a victim just as his allies alleged. The fact that the same tactics were attempted on Gilbert de la Porrée and failed because of the memory of Abelard demonstrates that the proceedings before and during the Council of Sens were carefully orchestrated to put Abelard at a disadvantage.

Those articles held against Abelard were summarized by Otto of Freising as being:

> That the Father has full power, the Son some power, the Holy Spirit no power; that the Holy Spirit is the world soul; that Christ did not become flesh to save us from the yoke of the devil; that they did not sin who crucified Christ in ignorance.[50]

In the face of such strong denunciations, it might appear that Abelard's followers offered him little support in his times of crisis, but that is not the actual case. That Abelard had a substantial following cannot be doubted, for Geoffrey, Bishop of Chartres, in his defense of Abelard at Soissons, warned the council then of the possible repercussion of a conviction. He is quoted in the Historia Calamitatum as having said that

> All of you . . . know that this man's teaching . . . and his intellectual ability have won him many followers and supporters wherever he has studied. He has greatly lessened the reputation both of his own teachers and of ours . . . and even if your judgement is deserved you will offend many people, and large numbers will rally to his defense . . .[51]

This is precisely what happened, so that it was because of public sentiment that Abelard was released from St. Medard.

> . . . the news spread and everyone who heard it began to condemn outright this wanton act of cruelty . . . and the legate publicly denounced the jealousy of the French in this affair.[52]

Even Abelard's rivals, Alberic and Lotulph, denied their part in the condemnation.

Among his influencial friends, Abelard depended upon the good will of Count Theobald of Troyes and Champagne. He found shelter in Theobald's territory when he fled from St. Denis in 1122[53] and wrote that the count was "overjoyed by my arrival and made every provision for me."[54] Of course, Abelard as a member of the minor nobility might well have anticipated a warm welcome. He later established the oratory of the Paraclete in Troyes, where the magnetism of his personality and the skill of his logic again accounted for the deluge of students who braved the elements to study at his school and provide for his needs.

> . . . my students provided . . . food, clothing, work on the land . . . and improved it by building in wood and stone.[55]

After the Council of Sens, perhaps the most notorious of Abelard's supporters by written word was Berengar of Poitiers. He was a student of Abelard's and wrote a tract entitled Apologeticus wherein he defended his master's teachings and gave a highly colored description of the machinations of Bernard prior to the Council's being opened. The lengthy tract began with a scathing denunciation of Bernard in which he was criticized as being vain and frivolous in his youth and a deceiver in "these modern times," one whom people believed to have a special place with God, but who was in reality a snake in hiding. Then came a

87

detailed description of the meeting prior to the Council's scheduled meeting with Abelard, when the capitula were agreed upon and condemned in advance by, according to Berengar, drunkards.

> After dinner Peter's book was brought in, and somebody was told to read it in a loud voice . . . Then the cups were saluted, the goblets filled, the wine praised, and the episcopal throats moistened . . . The fumes of it had so invaded their brains, that the eyes of all were drooping from sleep. Still the reader droned on; the assembly snored . . . So when the reader came upon some thorn-bush in Peter's field, he exclaimed to the deaf ears of the bishops, 'Damnatis?' Hardly awake at the last syllable, in a drowsy voice, and with hanging heads, they muttered 'Damnamus.' Others, however, roused by the noise of the damners, decapitated the word, and said . . . 'namus.'[56]

This was followed by an unpleasant attack on Bernard's sermons on the Song of Songs.

The pamphlet was not a great success--no doubt due to the heavy-handed style--and although he produced another tract which has not survived, he made no progress in promoting Abelard's cause. Instead, Berengar drew to himself the antagonism of influential persons for having insulted the members of the council which had included the king, Louis VII (1137-1180), "and Thibaud, the count palatine, and other nobles and countless numbers of the people."[57] Berengar fled to Cevennes, and it was not until c. 1150 that Robert of Melun resumed the protest in his Sentences.[58]

John of Salisbury hinted at a vigorous display of support for Abelard in the Historia Pontificalis when discussing the career of Arnold of Brescia. He stated that Arnold

together with Master Hyacinth, who is
now a cardinal, zealously fostered his
cause against the abbot of Clairvaux.
After Master Peter had set out for
Cluny, he remained at Paris on the Mount
Sainte Geneviève, exponding the scrip-
tures to scholars at the church of St.
Hilary where Peter had been lodged.[59]

Otto of Freising, in discussing the activities of Arnold, indicated that he was not one who
would gain a favorable hearing in Abelard's cause,
since he was "abounding . . . in profusion of word
than in the weight of his ideas . . . The minds of
such men are inclined to devise heresies . . . [60]
Bernard wrote to the pope of Arnold as being "the
shield bearer of . . . Abelard,"[61] and so it was
not a matter of surprise when Innocent II responded with a condemnation for them both.

The account of the Council of Sens as given
by John of Salisbury in his Historia Pontificalis
(c. 1164) indicates that Berengar's charges of un-
fairness against Bernard may have been founded on
truth when he wrote

Various opinions are held of the abbot
himself, some saying one thing and some
another, because he attacked the two
men most famous for their learning -
Peter Abelard and . . . Gilbert - and
pursued them with such zeal that he se-
cured the condemnation of Peter and only
just failed to have the other condemned.[62]

He went on to compare the series of events of Gilbert de la Porrée's case with those of Abelard's,
showing that in both cases the bishops had agreed
in advance that the errors presented by Bernard
were indeed unorthodox and condemned them as
such.[63] Although it was too late for Abelard, his
case was what later saved Gilbert, for

. . . the cardinals were very wrath with

89

the abbot and those who had assembled
at his request: they agreed among themselves to support the cause of the
bishop of Poitiers saying that the
abbot had attacked master Peter in ex-
actly the same way; but he had not had
access to the apostolic see, which was
accustomed to confound schemes of this
kind and snatch the weak from the
clutches of the strong.[64]

Protests to Abelard's condemnation were not
all as flamboyant as that of Berengar, but they
did exist. Magister Mainerius, who had been one
of Abelard's favorite students, saw the action of
the Council of Sens as a portent of the future of
the schools when he wrote, "Woe to the day when
law shall kill the study of letters . . . "[65] And
Hyacinth Baboni defended Abelard during the council and also promised to do so before the Curia in
Rome, but there is no record of his attempt[66] and
the pope's quick action in the case may have precluded further efforts. His defense of Abelard
did not affect his career, however, for in 1191 he
became Pope Celestine III.[67]

Robert of Melun defended one of Abelard's
views against Bernard's attack and cited St. John
Crysostum and pseudo-Jerome as his authorities.
He claimed that Abelard's use of the attributes of
Power, Wisdom, and Goodness for the three Persons
of the Trinity was justifiable, and wrote in his
Sentences (c. 1150) against those who are presump-
tuous while lacking in understanding:

it was an obstinate custom with such
people in matters of which they were ignorant to condemn others, without discussion and without rational enquiry.[68]

He also explained that

the fact that Power designates the Father
does not make him more powerful than
either the Son or the Spirit, while the

> power of the Spirit comes from both
> the other two Persons of the Trinity
> . . . The Generation of the Son and
> the Double Procession of the Spirit
> does not render them any the less om-
> nipotent than the Father.[69]

But of all of Abelard's supporters, the most
eloquent was that shown by the quiet council and
assistance offered to Abelard in his time of need
by Peter the Venerable. The abbot of Cluny was a
friend who had watched Abelard's career with great
interest. It is very likely that even before Abelard had entered St. Denis--and before he had met
Heloise--Peter the Venerable had urged Abelard to
leave the wealth and fame he had acquired from his
teaching in the schools and to come to Cluny.

> Why, my dear friend, do you frequent the
> schools? Why do you teach and try to
> teach? . . . Hath not God made foolish
> the wisdom of this world?[70]

The Peter to whom this letter was addressed seems
to have been Peter Abelard, for he was reminded
several times of the virtues of forsaking fame and
vain studies for the true peace of Cluny and the
deeper religious studies of a monastery. Peter
the Venerable gently admonished that "the kingdom
of God is not in word, but in power" and that the
poor in spirit gain the kingdom of heaven

> . . . without meditating on Plato, with-
> out academic disputations, without Aris-
> totelian snares, without philosophic
> doctrines . . .[71]

And after Abelard had progressed through his life
and had suffered defeat at Soissons and Sens,
Peter the Venerable welcomed him to Cluny as to a
safe harbor for a storm-tossed ship whose voyage
was nearly over. The abbot of Cluny sent the letter to Pope Innocent II telling of the reconciliation between Abelard and Bernard, and requesting
that Abelard be allowed to remain and teach at the

Cluniac monastery. He wrote that Abelard

> . . . went and . . . made his peace
> with the abbot of Clairvaux and . . .
> their previous differences were settled
> . . . Meanwhile . . . he decided to
> abandon the turmoil of schools and
> teaching and to remain permanently in
> your house of Cluny . . . in view of
> his age and weakness and his religious
> calling . . . we . . . granted his
> wish, and on condition that it is agree-
> able to your Holiness, we have willing-
> ly and gladly agreed that he shall re-
> main with us who, as you know, are
> wholly your own . . . [72]

A later letter written by Peter the Venerable to
Heloise indicated that the pope had given his con-
sent, and thus lifted the brand of heresy from
Abelard. He wrote that Abelard

> . . . was present at the holy Sacra-
> ments, offering the sacrifice of the
> immortal lamb to God whenever he could,
> and indeed, almost without interruption,
> after he had been restored to apostalic
> grace through my letter and efforts on
> his behalf.[73]

It was largely through the efforts of Peter
the Venerable that Abelard "did not pass into the
memory of posterity as an outcast but as a repent-
ant heretic and unfortunate man of genius"[74] who
found peace and a renewed spirit at the end of his
life. Indeed, the Abelard described by the abbot
of Cluny differed substantially from the Abelard
who had gathered throngs of admiring students
about him wherever he went and had aroused the
fear and envy of his rivals. He who had been denounced as conceited and proud was a changed man
at Cluny. Peter the Venerable wrote to Heloise
after her husband's death:

> I do not remember seeing anyone . . .

who was his equal in conduct and manner:
St. Germain could not have appeared more
lowly nor St. Martin himself so poor
. . . the shabbiness of his attire made
him look the humblest of . . . all . . .
I almost stood still in astonishment
that a man who bore so great and distinguished a name could thus humble and
abase himself.[75]

After a stormy career marked by two ecclesiastical councils, Abelard himself concluded that
"logic has made me hated by the world."[76] In his
"Confession of Faith," preserved and publicized by
Berengar of Poitiers, Abelard denounced the arguments used by his enemies to seek his condemnation,
and said these were arrived at "by conjecture
rather than weight of evidence."[77] But then, the
words of his adversaries indicate that their
greatest complaint against Abelard was that he
"draws the multitude after him."[78] Perhaps there
was cause for the fear of Abelard's influence on
the minds of his followers, for even John of Salis-
bury--noted for his moderation and tolerance--
wrote in his Policraticus (Statesman's Book)
against people who

fall into the error of thinking that
everything is a matter of the arbitrary
will and discretion of those who make
decisions, instead of being rather a
matter of truth and science.[79]

Abelard had been silenced, but his thought continued to live.

CHAPTER THREE FOOTNOTES

[1]Muckle, Adversities, Hist. Cal., p. 14.

[2]Ibid., p. 18.   [3]Ibid., p. 24.

[4]Ibid. Abelard attributed Anselm's hostility to the instigation of these two students.

[5]Otto of Freising and His Continuator, Rahewin, The Deeds of Frederick Barbarossa, trans. and annotated with an introduction by Charles Christopher Mierow (New York: Norton and Company, Inc., 1966), p. 83. Bishop Otto of Freising was the maternal uncle of Frederick Barbarossa and began a biography of the emperor in 1157 at his nephew's request. Although he followed the emperor's guidelines, Otto nevertheless included numerous digressions in which he commented upon the lives and activities of his contemporaries. He had studied in Paris around 1127 or 1128 and thus had some contact with the teachings of Abelard, but it is unknown whether or not he attended any of Abelard's lectures.

[6]Muckle, Adversities, Hist. Cal., p. 40.

[7]Otto of Freising, The Deeds of Frederick Barbarossa, p. 83. Abelard is described as "holding to the doctrine of nominalism in natural philosophy . . . (and) rashly carried it over into theology."

[8]Abelard, The Letters of Abelard and Heloise, trans. Radice, p. 79.

[9]Otto of Freising, The Deed of Frederick

94

Barbarossa, p. 83. Sabellius, a third century African priest, overemphasized the unity of the three Persons of the Trinity.

[10]Ibid.   [11]Ibid., p. 84.

[12]Ibid. "No opportunity of making a reply was granted him because his skill in disputation was mistrusted by all."

[13]Sikes, Peter Abailard, p. 150. Abelard restated his opposition to Gilbert de la Porrée's theories in his Theologia Christiana, again using Augustine's de Trinitate for his authority.

[14]Abelard, The Letters of Abelard and Heloise, trans. Radice, p. 80. (Hist. Cal.)

[15]Ibid.   [16]Ibid., p. 82.

[17]Ibid., p. 83. Abelard stated that the bishop of Chartres told him the legate "was only acting under pressure and would set me quite free within a few days of his leaving Soissons."

[18]Étienne Gilson, The Spirit of Mediaeval Philosophy (Gifford Lectures 1931-1932), trans. A.H.C. Downes (New York: Charles Scribner's Sons, 1940), p. 13.

[19]Guibert of Nogent, Self and Society in Medieval France. The Memoirs of Abbot Guibert of Nogent (1064?-c. 1125), trans. with an introduction and notes by John F. Benton (New York: Harper and Row, Harper Torchbooks, 1970), p. 20. This section was quoted by the editor in the introduction to Guibert's Memoirs.

[20]Luscombe, The School of Peter Abelard, p. 11. The author cites Clarembald's Commentary on Boethius' De Trinitate, ed. Jansen, p. 48.

[21]Bernard of Clairvaux, Studies Presented to Dom Jean Leclerq, pp. 70-71. The Ransom Theory is found in proposition 7.

[22]Sikes, Peter Abailard, p. 241, the author's analysis of Walter's writing.

[23]Ibid., p. 226. Taken from Epistle IV of Hugo's Sacrae Antiquitatis Monumenta.

[24]Philippe Delhaye, Medieval Christian Philosophy, trans. S.J. Tester (New York: Hawthorne Books, Publishers, 1960), p. 68. The treatise is referred to as a diatribe.

[25]St. Bernard of Clairvaux. His Life as Recorded in the Vita Prima Bernardi by William of St. Thierry, Arnold of Bonnevaux, Geoffrey and Philip of Clairvaux, and Odo of Deuil (London: A. R. Mowbray and Company, Limited, 1959), p. 100. Trans. Adrian Walker and Geoffrey Webb. From Geoffrey's Book Three. Geoffrey was Abbot of Clairvaux ten years after St. Bernard's death.

[26]Burch, Early Medieval Philosophy, p. 78. From Abelard's Theologia Christiana.

[27]Sikes, Peter Abailard, p. 155. From William of St. Thierry's Disputatio Adversus Abelardsum. William refers to the seal as copper rather than bronze, thus making it a matter of conjecture as to whether or not he had Abelard's work before him when he wrote his objections, or had merely heard of the analogy from someone and had responded to hearsay, or if the metal has been mis-translated.

[28]Ibid.

[29]Ibid., p. 157. The complaint was based on Abelard's use of the attributes of Power, Wisdom, and Goodness when describing the Persons of the Trinity.

[30]Vita Prima Bernardi, trans. Walker and Webb, p. 100.

[31]Ibid.

^{32}Helen Waddell, The Wandering Scholars, 7th ed. (London: Constable and Company, Limited, 1927; revised and reprint ed., 1966), p. 118. The author quoted from Remusat, Abelard, p. 185. "Dilexi et ego eum." S. Bernard, Epistle 326.

^{33}Otto of Freising, Deeds of Frederick Barbarossa, p. 82.

^{34}Thomas Merton, The Last of the Fathers. Saint Bernard of Clairvaux and the Encyclical Letter, "Doctor Mellifluus" (New York: Harcourt, Brace and Company, 1954), pp. 57-58. From Bernard's Contra Errores Abelardi.

^{35}Vita Prima Bernardi, trans. Walker and Webb, p. 101.

^{36}Ibid. Geoffrey of Clairvaux recorded the account of this meeting.

^{37}Ibid.

^{38}Morison, The Life and Times of St. Bernard, p. 279. Abelard's innovation was to use St. Matthew's "super-substantial bread" rather than inserting the "daily bread" of St. Luke's version. St. Bernard, however, was equally unpleasant and referred to Abelard in a letter to a cardinal as "a monk without a rule, a prelate without responsibility, an abbot without discipline, who argues with boys and consorts with women." (See St. Bernard of Clairvaux, Letters, p. 325. Letter 244 to Cardinal G.)

^{39}Vita Prima Bernardi, trans. Walker and Webb, p. 101. Geoffrey of Clairvaux attributes Abelard's change of heart to his "being persuaded by his own great talents and the evil counsels of certain of his confreres, that he could defend his position by the force of his own arguments."

^{40}Ibid., p. 102.

[41]Bernard of Clairvaux: Studies Presented to
Dom Jean Leclercq, pp. 68-69.

[42]Vita Prima Bernardi, trans. Walker and Webb,
p. 102.

[43]Ibid.

[44]Sikes, Peter Abailard, p. 235.

[45]Otto of Freising, The Deeds of Frederick
Barbarossa, p. 84. Otto quotes all the correspondence involved in this affair.

[46]Ibid., p. 85. Quoting from Bernard's letter
to Innocent II.

[47]Vita Prima Bernardi, trans. Walker and Webb,
p. 102. Geoffrey of Clairvaux quotes from Bernard's letter to Innocent II on Abelard's errors.
He indicates that Bernard sent his compilation of
the errors prior to Sens.

[48]Otto of Freising, The Deeds of Frederick
Barbarossa, p. 87. Quoting Pope Innocent II's
reply to the bishops and Bernard.

[49]Ibid. [50]Ibid., p. 88.

[51]Abelard, The Letters of Abelard and Heloise,
trans. Radice, p. 81. From the Historia Calamitatum.

[52]Ibid., p. 85. Hist. Cal.

[53]Ibid., p. 87. Hist. Cal. The year of Abelard's departure from St. Denis may be figured by
the year Suger became abbot.

[54]Ibid. Hist. Cal. [55]Ibid., p. 90, Hist. Cal.

[56]Morison, The Life and Times of St. Bernard,
pp. 315-316, quoting from the Apology of Berengarius.

[57]Otto of Freising, The Deeds of Frederick Barbarossa, p. 84. Otto makes it clear that Bernard had spoken to the crowds against Abelard's teachings, but also states that Abelard's followers included "a very great throng of purple."

[58]Sikes, Peter Abailard, p. 238.

[59]John of Salisbury, Memoirs of the Papal Court, trans. Marjorie Chibnall (London: Thomas Nelson and Sons, Limited, 1956, reprint ed. 1965), pp. 63-64. The Hyacinth mentioned was Hyacinth Orsini, Cardinal-Deacon of St. Mary in Cosmedin, who died March 8, 1144. John of Salisbury's work is also called the Historia Pontificalis.

[60]Otto of Freising, The Deeds of Frederick Barbarossa, p. 143.

[61]Luscombe, The School of Peter Abelard, p. 26. Luscombe suspects that Abelard's association with Arnold of Brescia may have caused him to be thought of as "an anti-clerical free-thinker."

[62]John of Salisbury, Memoirs of the Papal Court, p. 16.

[63]Ibid., p. 20. Chibnall presents a brief discussion in n. 1 concerning the drawing up of a capitula prior to the council's meeting and St. Bernard's role in having this condemned in advance.

[64]Ibid., pp. 19-20.

[65]Waddell, The Wandering Scholars, p. 144.

[66]Sikes, Peter Abailard, p. 239.

[67]Luscombe, The School of Peter Abelard, p. 23, Hyacinth Baboni became a cardinal shortly after Abelard's death, and in 1191 was made pope and took the name Celestine III.

[68]Ibid., p. 287, quoting from Robert of Melun,

<u>Sentences</u>. He may have composed this work as late as the early 1160's, and he died in 1167.

[69]Sikes, <u>Peter Abailard</u>, p. 162, quoting from Robert of Melun's <u>Sentences</u>.

[70]Peter the Venerable, <u>The Letters of Peter the Venerable</u>, ed. Giles Constable with introduction and notes, vol. 2 (Cambridge, Massachusetts: Harvard University Press 1967), p. 102, quoting from Letter 9, vol. 1, p. 16, written to an unspecified Peter.

[71]Ibid.

[72]Abelard, <u>The Letters of Abelard and Heloise</u>, trans. Radice, pp. 275-276. This quote is taken from Radice's translation of Letter 98 from Constable, <u>Letters of Peter the Venerable</u>, written to Pope Innocent II.

[73]Ibid., p. 282, quoting Letter 115 from Constable, <u>Letters of Peter the Venerable</u>, written to Heloise at the Paraclete.

[74]Luscombe, <u>The School of Peter Abelard</u>, p. 20.

[75]Abelard, <u>The Letters of Abelard and Heloise</u>, trans. Radice, p. 282, quoting from Letter 115 from Constable, <u>Letters of Peter the Venerable</u>, written to Heloise.

[76]Ibid., p. 270, quoting from Abelard's "Confession of Faith," which was written to Heloise.

[77]Ibid.

[78]Otto of Freising, <u>The Deeds of Frederick Barbarossa</u>, p. 85, quoting from Bernard's letter to Pope Innocent II.

[79]John of Salisbury, <u>The Statesman's Book of John of Salisbury</u>, trans. John Dickinson (New York: Russell and Russell, 1963), p. 100. While he was quoting from Cicero's <u>De Officiis,</u> the last

100

clause was his own addition and shows the influence
Abelard had upon John of Salisbury.

CHAPTER FOUR

ABELARD'S INFLUENCE ON THE FOUNDING OF

THE UNIVERSITY OF PARIS AND

THE RISE OF SCHOLASTICISM

The twelfth century was a turning point in
the European system of education which had previously emphasized only the limited study of grammar
and dialectic. These studies became insufficient
and were overshadowed by the revival of the complete trivium of grammar, logic, and rhetoric, and
the quadrivium of mathematics, geometry, astronomy, and music. The center of attention soon
shifted to philosophy with the major interest being in determining the difference between the elements of philosophy. This study of logic, ethics,
physics, and later metaphysics, was cultivated and
was eventually introduced into the area of theology,[1] resulting in the creation of numerous commentaries on the scriptures and the development of
the collections of Sentences (cpinions) and the
Summae (summaries). Since these collections followed a logical organization, theology gradually
became systematized like a science.[2]

Peter Abelard was at the forefront of the educational changes of the twelfth century. His
teaching method was absorbed by his numerous students and was carried into the thirteenth century
where it formed the basis for scholasticism. Abelard considered reason and philosophy to be valid
tools of theology since they were given to men by
God, and thus he boldly espoused the idea once
held by St. Anselm that faith and reason were both

103

proper avenues to truth. But whereas St. Anselm
later altered his opinions to emphasize faith and
make reason simply a means of discourse in matters
of faith,[3] Abelard re-emphasized the value of reason for understanding one's faith and for convinc-
ing others of the truth of Christianity.

Abelard often turned to St. Augustine for support in his use of reason since Augustine had
called upon reason for studying the scriptures and
for determining what was orthodox and what was
heretical.[4] Abelard's dialectical method, however, was employed to stimulate thought and en-
courage a questioning attitude in his students
rather than to make a judgment. His primary concern was that his students search for truth.[5] In
his Sic et Non, Abelard said,

> . . . This questioning excites young
> readers to the maximum of effort in
> inquiring into the truth, and such in-
> quiry sharpens their minds. Assiduous
> and frequent questioning is indeed the
> first key to wisdom . . . for by
> doubting we come to inquiry; through
> inquiring we perceive the truth . . .[6]

Because of his method of teaching, Abelard
was a liberator of the human intellect. The nov-
elty of Abelard's theories and methods induced a
powerful opposition to rise against it. Abelard
was considered by St. Bernard of Clairvaux and
William of St. Thierry to be a threat to faith and
he was subsequently denounced by them for daring
to subject divine matters to the scrutiny of reason.[7]

In his Sic et Non, Abelard presented conflicting statements by St. Augustine and the
Church Fathers on such dogmatic propositions as
the oneness of God, the infinite aspect of the
Son, the ability of God to do all things, the
equality of the apostles, the need for a baptism
of water for salvation, and the importance of good
works for salvation. In all, he presented 156

quotations with arguments for and against. This
same method was later used by Gratian when he composed his Concord of Discordant Canons (c. 1148),
which systematized church laws, customs, and papal
decrees to 1139, and was further supported by the
introduction to Christian Europe of Aristotle's
Logica nova and Topics in the thirteenth century.[9]
By the end of the thirteenth century, Abelard's
method of disputation was an integral part of
scholasticism as bolstered by Peter Lombard's
Sententiarum libri IV in 1150 and epitomized by
the twenty-one volume Summa theologica of St.
Thomas Aquinas written between 1267 and 1273.[10]

Abelard's classroom techniques was lively and
entertaining, and encouraged his students to exper-
iment with new approaches and new ideas.[11] He in-
tegrated the traditional use of commentaries with
an orderly study of theology based on logical subject groupings which emphasized the use of reason
and rational methods.[12] But Abelard did not himself ignore authority. Instead, he confined his
solutions to a technical orthodoxy, while opening
the way for others to assume an even greater degree of liberty in their rational explorations of
the mysteries of faith.[13] Abelard's students produced ten or eleven theological summae utilizing
the categories Abelard had stressed for salvation:
faith, charity (virtues), and the sacraments.
These topics formed the core of Abelard's Introductio ad theologia and had been borrowed, in turn,
from St. Augustine.[14] The works of Abelard's students were the start of the intellectual movement
that would ensure the success of dialectic and
systematized theology in the thirteenth century.[15]
Thus, the influence of Abelard's teaching and the
magnetism of his personality, which drew thousands
of students to Paris, turned that city into the
intellectual center of France.

The influx of students to Paris continued after Abelard's death. His presence had increased
the fame of the Paris schools and his methods continued to flourish there. The abbey of Ste. Gene-
vieve, where Abelard had taught during his last

years in Paris prior to the Council of Sens, came under the control of the canons of St. Victor and the school was reformed for the exclusive theological needs of the Augustinian canons.[17]

At the time that Abelard taught in Paris, the city boasted of three main schools. There was the cathedral school of Notre Dame, the school of Ste. Geneviève, and the abbey of St. Victor, which had been established in 1108 by William of Champeaux. St. Victor's ceased to be a school by the thirteenth century, and after Ste. Geneviève became solely a religious school for Augustinian canons, it too declined. The University of Paris may be traced to the school of Notre Dame in that only its chancellor could license teachers in the diocese.[18] Abelard had established himself without the required license on Mount Ste. Geneviève in 1108, but became attached to Notre Dame in 1113, as he wrote in his Historia Calamitatum:

> . . . I returned to Paris, to the school which had long ago been intended for and offered to me, and from which I had been expelled at the start.[19]

The development of the University of Paris came about through now obscure stages, but Ste. Geneviève and Notre Dame both figured predominantly in its formation.[20] The University was founded in 1200 by Philip II of France and came from the schools of Abelard's time on the left bank of the Seine and the cathedral school where Abelard's student, Peter Lombard, taught.[21] It was sometime around 1210 that Pope Innocent III issued a bull recognizing and approving the statutes of the teacher's guild which had been established in the area about 1170. The guild was later authorized to send a proctor to the papal court to represent its interests, and it is therefore difficult to ascertain the exact beginnings of the University of Paris.[22]

Abelard's talent as an instructor and his love for controversy were both important factors

106

in the increase and expansion of studies at Paris as well as in the growth of the intellectual movement that resulted in the formation of the University of Paris.[23] His teaching of theology and philosophy was highly successful, and he described the resulting fame he had acquired at the outset of his career in the Historia Calamitatum: "The numbers in the school increased enormously as the students gathered there eager for instruction in both subjects, . . ."[24]

The fact that Abelard originally opened his school without a license from Notre Dame anticipated the future trend wherein the University would come to displace or absorb the episcopal schools. By the mid-thirteenth century, the University of Paris excluded monks from the faculty of arts and supported the French kings over the papacy.[25] The universities of the thirteenth century were protected by both ecclesiastical and secular powers and gained the majority of the students as a result. Thus, the secular universities came to represent progressive ideas and passed the older schools.[26] When Abelard received permission to establish his oratory in the wilderness, it was to the King, Louis the Fat, and his minister, Stephen de Garlande, that he made his appeal. His abbot, Suger, acquiesced in this arrangement on the condition that Abelard not attach himself to any other monastery. This protection granted by the king and his minister to a man who had already been condemned at Soissons may be considered an early example of the privileges that would be granted in the thirteenth century to universities by secular rulers.[27]

In Paris, Abelard attracted more than five thousand students to his school, and by his teaching he raised the intellectual standards of his day.[28] His school was opened to anyone who cared to attend,[29] and consequently his students included not only twenty cardinals, fifty archbishops and bishops, and one pope (Celestine II), but also the revolutionary, Arnold of Brescia, and the even-tempered John of Salisbury.[30] Abelard's

method of instruction became the model for future
studies in the sciences, theology, and the liberal
arts for the University of Paris.[31]

Abelard's influence on the founding of the
University of Paris extended beyond merely his
ability to attract masses of students to the city
from the diverse parts of Europe. He also popu-
larized the methods and courses of study which became the staple of the University for several centuries. It was Abelard who brought reason to
theology and prepared the way for abstract philosophy.[32] Because Abelard dared to introduce a new
approach to education and philosophy, he led the
way to the liberation of thought which was developed in the Renaissance and further realized in
the spirit of rationalism. The far-reaching ef-
fects of Abelard's teaching may be seen in the
University of Paris--of which he must necessarily
be considered a founder--which came to serve as
the model for other European universities through
the Renaissance.[33]

To understand the significance of Abelard's
instruction in the light of the future courses of
study followed by Medieval universities, it is important to accord to him a prominent place in the
development of scholasticism and to recognize him
as the one dominant figure of the twelfth century
who anticipated the philosophy of Aristotle, and
even formulated what may be considered the first
attempt at a genuine Christian philosophy.[34] Abelard's influence in these areas survived his condemnation at Sens and continued to provide a stim-
ulus to thought long after his death.

Scholasticism as the method of subjecting
theology to scrutinization by logic and using reason to explain dogma,[35] was continued by Abelard's
followers after Sens. The school at Mount Ste.
Geneviève was fused with the school of Hugh of St.
Victor's when Abelard's students incorporated Vic-
torine criticism and direction into their work.
Abelard's writings were not forgotten, but initiated debate and stimulated more thought. From the

school of St. Victor's came constructive criticisms of Abelard which showed how greatly he inspired creative thought.[36] The theological compo-
sitions produced by Abelard's school show the
development of early scholastic logic and theology, and included The Sentences of Abelard (1150)
of Roland Bandinelli, future Pope Alexander III,
and the Sentences of Master Omnibene, later Bishop
of Verona.[37]

Abelard's successors continued his practice
of citing patristic and scriptural sources and
used these to enhance their conclusions or to re-
inforce their positions on issues.[38] This use of
quotations became even more prevalent in the
school of Hugh of St. Victor after it merged with
that of Ste. Geneviève, and reason was blended into this otherwise conservative background.[39] The
system of scholastic presentation fit the pattern
established by Abelard. Moral theology, as presented in the Sententiae Parisienses and the Sententiae Hermani of Abelard's school, commenced
with the consideration of virtues as related to
charity, for virtue was seen as dependent upon
charity, and was contrasted with its opposite,
vice and sin. The conclusion consisted of a study
of merit and the conditions which affect it,[40] and
thus echoes the style used by Abelard in his Scito
te Ipsum.

Dialectic continued to be used to draw together philosophy and theology in matters of
ethics. In 1160, the term "moral theology" was
introduced for the first time by Alain of Lille in
his De virtutibus et vitiis (On Virtues and Vices)
wherein he questioned the value of philosophical
virtues for Christians.[41] The preoccupations with
patristic and scriptural quotations is especially
apparent in Peter Lombard's Sententiarum Libri IV,
which became the backbone of Medieval scholasticism. Indeed, almost twenty years after Abelard's
death, Gerhoh of Reichersberg--who had compared
Abelard's followers to the locusts of the Apoca-
lypse--lamented that these disciples had infested
the schools of France and Germany.[42] St. Thomas

Aquinas also carried on in the tradition of Abelard and brought the scholastic method to its apex
by 1273.   After St. Thomas, the method became more
important than the content.   St. Thomas' work, the
Summa theologica, had carried scholasticism to its
fullest potential as an intellectual tool; and because successive generations held fast to this
masterpiece, it came to stifle rather than liberate the intellect.[43]

Through the twelfth and thirteenth centuries
there was a conflict between Christian theology
and pagan philosophy.   Abelard initiated this fric-
tion by applying the Aristotelian method of inquiry to theology in his attempt to formulate a
Christian philosophy.   The Logica nova of Aristotle had become assimilated by the end of the
twelfth century, and was followed by Aristotle's
Metaphysics in the thirteenth century.   This work
and the Arabic commentaries were purged of errors
by order of the pope in 1231, and by 1254, were
incorporated into the curriculum at the University
of Paris and reconciled to Christianity.[44]   Abelard's use of dialectic in theology resulted in
his condemnation at Sens, but soon after, in 1140,
Thierry of Chartres produced the Heptateuchon in
which the whole of Aristotle's logic was introduced.   The initial shock of Abelard's use of
logic was past, and now theologians began to apply
Aristotle to theology.[45]

The influx of Aristotle replaced the Neo-
Platonistic outlook of Christianity with the idea
of practical wisdom and the blending of the scientific with the philosophical.[46]   Abelard had
perceived the dual levels of Aristotle's logic in
his own exploration of the concept of universals.
He had gone beyond the logical level which was il-
lustrated by nominalism and had touched upon the
metaphysical when he added the truth of a subject
to its word.   Abelard, therefore, passed from
merely discerning the object to sensing its innate
reality.[47]   Twelfth century writers came to include the pagan ethics in the area of rhetoric and
grammar, and after Abelard, ethics was

110

incorporated into the area of theology. But again, the impetus came from Abelard who placed the ethics of the pagans alongside the theology of the Christians, where the ethics were reconciled to God while admittedly generating from man.[48]

During the twelfth century, the application of dialectic to Christian theology became more apparent as writers began to attempt a formulation of a genuine Christian philosophy. There were those who battled against this trend and sought to prevent the inclusion of pagan reasoning into Christianity. St. Peter Damian, St. Bernard of Clairvaux, William of St. Thierry, and Walter of St. Victor all held to intuition and piety rather than reason and intellectual scholarship as the proper means of seeking God and salvation.[49] In his <u>Scito te Ipsum</u>, Abelard brought dialectic to theology in the area of ethics and there fought against the moral theory of his time. He emphasized the intention over the act, making sin a matter of the subjective mind rather than of the deed.[50] Abelard went further from this, however, and indicated in his <u>Theologia Christiana</u> that the pagan philosophers were divinely inspired about the Trinity and were therefore worthy of salvation. He wrote:

> . . . First of all, however, I must show that this distinction of Persons in the divine Trinity did not begin with Christ, but was handed on more clearly and carefully by Him. The divine inspiration, in fact, revealed the Trinity by the prophets to the Jews and by the philosophers to the Gentiles, . . . So, too, it was posssible for this faith in the Trinity to be more easily adopted in the time of grace by both Jews and Gentiles, seeing that they could trace its course from the ancient learned men.[51]

St. Bernard, however, saw this claim as a challenge to the genuineness of Christian truth.[52]

Even in the blending of pagan and Christian thought, Abelard maintained his references to authority. In his Theologia Christiana, Abelard first mentioned the predictions of the pagan Sibylline prophetess, but then cited St. Augustine's similar acknowledgement of the Christian content of these oracles.[53] He further attempted to show the universality of the Christian Trinitarian belief by mentioning the similarities in the tenets of the Hindu Brahmins.[54]

In comparing pagan thought to Christian belief, Abelard interchanged certain terms and attributed an orthodoxy to pagan expressions. The World Soul of Plato was equated to the Christian Holy Spirit, and Jewish terminology was adapted to the Christian Trinity so that the Father, Son, and Holy Spirit were compared to the Old Testament references of Power, Wisdom, and Goodness. In the Theologia Christiana, Abelard stated that Plato

> . . . says that the anima mundi, or soul of the world, was either begotten or had its existence from God before the foundation of the world. Unless I am much mistaken, we can detect in these words the perpetual procession of the Holy Spirit from God the Father.[55]

He supported his terminology for the Trinity with quotes from the Psalms, Ecclesiastes, Genesis, and Proverbs. For Power, Abelard cited Genesis for the creation of all things by God the Father. For Wisdom, Abelard wrote:

> . . . We find clearly in Ecclesiasticus that the Word of God must be understood as His wisdom: 'All wisdom is from the Lord God, and was ever with Him from the beginning . . . Wisdom was created before all things and the understanding of wisdom from the first. The fount of wisdom is the Word of God' . . .[56]

Then, from Proverbs, Abelard used:

112

I, wisdom, dwell in counsel. The
Lord hath possessed me from the beginning of His ways before He created
anything from the first.[57]

The Holy Spirit as Goodness was supported by quoting from Psalms:

Thy good spirit shall lead me in the
right way.[58]

But Abelard also bolstered his arguments with numerous quotes from St. Augustine's City of God,
Against Five Heresies, and On the Trinity, lest
anyone object to his sources.

Nevertheless, Abelard's theological theories
were repudiated by St. Bernard who felt that the
attributes of Power, Wisdom, and Goodness resulted
in a disunity in the Godhead, making only the
Father powerful.[59] Abelard's students compounded
the misunderstandings by oversimplifying his arguments in their own commentaries while being unable
to match his skill in the use of precise speech.[60]
The writings of his followers were attributed to
his teaching, and thus Abelard was condemned at
Sens not only for his own misinterpreted statements, but also for the statements of his pupils.
The discrepancies between Abelard's teaching and
the commentaries of his students must have been
obvious to Abelard's contemporaries. They were
familiar with Abelard's skill in disputation and
the care with which he worded his writings, and so
it may have been that the writings of his students
were not so much considered as proof of the criticism leveled against Abelard by his critics, but
as evidence of the danger of too much liberty of
thought.[61]

Although later writers rejected many of Abelard's theological points, they did take the time
to compile negative criticisms of his ideas.[62]
But while this was true, some of Abelard's doctrines were kept, purged of heresy, by Peter Lombard, Omnibene, and Roland Bandinelli. Abelard's

ideas on what he considered the three theological
necessities for salvation (faith, charity, and the
sacraments) and his analogy of the bronze (or copper) seal to illustrate the generation of the Son
and the Double Procession of the Holy Spirit were
included in their works. They also retained Abelard's concept of faith as existimatio ("judgment"
rather than the "opinion" denounced by St. Bernard), and used his doctrine of the Trinity with
its attributes of Power, Wisdom, and Goodness.
They agreed with his definition of Original Sin as
being the guilt inherited from Adam's sin, and
agreed at least in part with Abelard's view of the
Atonement.[63] Both Peter Lombard and St. Thomas
Aquinas emphasized Christ's humilty rather than
Adam's pride and thus contributed to the decline
of the Ransom Theory of the Atonement.[64]

In his attempt at bridging pagan philosophy
and Christian theology, Abelard was accused by St.
Bernard of writing things "that are novel and
profane both in their wording and in their
sense."[65] Bernard's attack was stated in a series
of letters to the pope and various cardinals in
1140, and showed that his greatest concern was
that Abelard accepted no limitations to his intellectual pursuit of truth. To Cardinal Ivo, Bernard wrote about Abelard:

> . . . He corrupts the integrity of the
> faith and the chastity of the Church.
> He oversteps the landmarks placed by
> our Fathers in discussing and writing
> about faith, the sacraments, and the
> Holy Trinity; . . . In his books and
> in his works he shows himself to be a
> fabricator of falsehood, a coiner of
> perverse dogmas, proving himself a
> heretic not so much by his error as by
> his obstinate defence of error. He is
> a man who does not know his limitations
> . . .[66]

In his letter to Pope Innocent II, Bernard's ap-
prehension was based upon the far-reaching

implications of Abelard's method. Bernard wrote
concerning Abelard:

> It is not wonderful if a man who cares
> not what his words may mean should rush
> in upon the hidden things of faith, and
> thus profanely invade and despoil the
> concealed treasures of devotion, seeing
> that he has no feeling either of piety
> or allegiance to the faith. At the
> very commencement of his 'Theology,' or
> rather Fool-ology, he defines faith as
> being opinion. As if any one might
> think or say what pleased him concern-
> ing it; . . . These ideas and opinions
> belong to the Academics, who doubt of
> all things and know nothing.[67]

St. Bernard had thus perceived the true danger of Abelard's unconventional application of
reason to theology as the initial impetus towards
a new theological and philosophical outlook. In
this respect, Abelard's Christian philosophy provided the foundation for the later development of
philosophical rationalism.

Abelard's teachings denoted his belief that
men were justified in their reliance upon reason,
but he was himself careful to maintain the impos-
sibility of knowing God through pure reason. He
wrote in his Theologia Christiana:

> . . . The Lord alone knows the truth.
> I consider that I shall set forth that
> which is like the truth and most agrees
> with philosophical reasons. If in
> doing this, owing to my own shortcomings,
> I diminish catholic understanding or
> expressions (which God forbid!) then let
> God, Who judges works by their inten-
> tions, pardon me.[68]

Abelard was, above all else, a Christian. In his
"Confession of Faith," he emphasized, "I do not
wish to be a philosopher if it means conflicting

with Paul."[69] But by opening the minds of his
students to the spirit of inquiry, Abelard allowed
rationalism to take root.

Abelard touched upon the relation between the
truths of the sacred writings and those of reason
in his <u>Dialectica</u>, and in his <u>Sic et Non</u>, he demonstrated that reason was needed to interpret the
scriptures and patristic writings. He used the
<u>Dialogus inter Philosophum, Judaeum, et Christian-
um</u> to project his theory that in Christianity
there was the perfection of the natural law of the
philosopher and the development of the Mosaic law
of the Jew.[70] His various works on Christian
theology stressed the elements of Christian truth
that could be found in the reasoning of pagan
philosophers. The Abelard who found between realism and nominalism the middle ground of conceptualism was also the Abelard who found in Christianity the synthesis of pagan philosophy and Jewish
religious tradition.

CHAPTER FOUR FOOTNOTES

[1]D.J.B. Hawkins, A Sketch of Mediaeval Philosophy (New York: Greenwood Press, Publishers, 1968), p. 60.

[2]Ibid., p. 61.

[3]Ibid., p. 70. Hawkins points out that the chronology of St. Anselm's writings shows the trend from the Monologion, where reason is used to "demonstrate the mystery of the Trinity" to the Proslogion, where his proof for God's existence was corrected and reason was used instead to confirm faith, and finally, to the use of reason as the means of extracting and discussing "the richness of revealed doctrine."

[4]Ibid., p. 74. St. Augustine considered prayer important, but also believed that one must attempt to understand scriptures by the use of one's own reason.

[5]Tierney, Sources of Medieval History, p. 147, from Abelard's prologue to the Sic et Non.

[6]Ibid.

[7]Gabriel Compayré, Abelard and the Origin and Early History of Universities (New York: Greenwood Press, Publishers, 1949), p. 19.

[8]Tierney, Sources of Medieval History, p. 148, from Abelard's Sic et Non.

[9]Charles Homer Haskins, The Rise of Universities, Brown University (New York: Henry Holt and

117

Company, 1923), p. 55.

[10]De Wulf, <u>History of Mediaeval Philosophy</u>, trans. Messenger, p. 202.

[11]Abelard's approach may be observed from the style of his <u>Sic et Non</u>.

[12]Hawkins, <u>A Sketch of Mediaeval Philosophy</u>, p. 74. Hawkins mentions that Abelard most likely obtained his teaching license at Melun or Paris after his return there from Anselm's school in Laon.

[13]Compayré, <u>Abelard and the Origin of Universities</u>, pp. 20-21.

[14]Hawkins, <u>A Sketch of Mediaeval Philosophy</u>, p. 75. The categories of faith and charity include dogma and morals respectively.

[15]Ibid.

[16]Leff, <u>Medieval Thought</u>, p. 107. By the time the cathedral was completed at Chartres, the city had eclipsed as the center of studies and Paris had taken its place. Abelard's presence in Paris was a major force in drawing students away from Chartres and other schools in France.

[17]Sikes, <u>Peter Abailard</u>, p. 247. The school at Ste. Geneviève was reformed in 1147 by Cluniacs prior to becoming a part of the school of St. Victor. Sikes points out that Abelard left no lasting school of theology in Paris and that none of his students carried on his school. However, Abelard's methods did not vanish but became incorporated into other schools.

[18]Haskins, <u>The Rise of Universities</u>, p. 21. See also Knowles, <u>The Evolution of Medieval Thought</u>, p. 163.

[19]Abelard, <u>The Letters of Abelard and Heloise</u>, trans. Radice, pp. 64-65, Hist. Cal. In n. 3,

p. 64, Radice indicates that Abelard at this time became a <u>magister scholarum</u> (master of rhetoric) at Notre Dame, and thus had acquired the necessary license to teach.

[20]Compayré, <u>Abelard and the Origin of Universities</u>, p. 14. According to Burch, <u>Early Medieval Philosophy</u>, p. 56, the school that Abelard set up on Mount Ste. Geneviève led to "the tradition of that 'Latin Quarter' which soon became the intellectual center of Europe."

[21]Leff, <u>Medieval Thought</u>, p. 178. Leff also states that the University of Paris became "the great center of logic, metaphysics, and theology, and the archetype of the 'masters' university.'"

[22]Will Durant, <u>The Story of Civilization</u>, vol. 4: <u>The Age of Faith</u> (New York: Simon and Schuster, 1950) p. 920. Durant notes that the schools which came to form the University of Paris had their first unity in the licensing of masters and initially had no special university buildings.

[23]Compayré, <u>Abelard and the Origin of Universities</u>, p. 4. The author draws this from Victor Cousin's introduction to his <u>Ouvrages inedits d'Abelard</u> (1836).

[24]Abelard, <u>The Letters of Abelard and Heloise</u>, trans. Radice, p. 65, Hist. Cal.

[25]Compayré, <u>Abelard and the Origin of Universities</u>, p. 7. By the mid-thirteenth century, the University of Paris excluded monks from the faculty of arts and supported the French kings over the papacy.

[26]Ibid., p. 8.

[27]Ibid., p. 15. The University of Paris had its own court to try cases involving its students, for example.

[28]Knowles, <u>The Evolution of Medieval Thought</u>,

p. 129. See Compayré in cited work, p. 17, for the numbers of students attending Abelard's classes.

[29]Compayré, Abelard and the Origin of Universities, p. 17. Compayré recounts an episode from the Vita Gosvini involving St. Gosvin when he was a student of William of Champeaux in 1108. He attempted to engage Abelard in a debate during his lecture only to be told to keep still and not interrupt--he was welcomed as a student.

[30]Ibid., p. 22. Pope Celestine II was Guy of Castello, a student of Abelard who was consecrated pope on September 26, 1143. See Luscombe, The School of Peter Abelard, pp. 15 and 23 for references to two other followers of Abelard who became popes. Luscombe mentions Roland Bandinelli--later Pope Alexander III who wrote The Sentences of Abelard in 1150--and Hyacinth Baboni--who became Pope Celestine III in 1191. These last two men were not students of Abelard, but supporters.

[31]Ibid., p. 4. Compayré cites in n. 3, Heinrich Denifle, editor of the Chartularium Universitatis Parisiensis C.U.P. (Paris: Delalain, 1889), t.i. Introduction, p. xvi. Compayre does not consider the schools of Rheims, Tours, Angers, and Laon as the direct origins of the University of Paris, but believes they may be better classed as a preparatory stage in the development of the University. (See Compayre, pp. 5-6.)

[32]Ibid., p. 22.   [33]Ibid., p. 3.

[34]Peter Abelard, Abelard's Christian Theology, trans. McCallum, p. 4, from McCallum's introduction. Further references to this work will be cited as Abelard, Abelard's Christian Theology.

[35]Compayré, Abelard and the Origin of Universities, p. 19. The author states that scholasticism had begun prior to Abelard, but that it became successful and prominent because Abelard promoted the scholastic method.

[36]Luscombe, The School of Peter Abelard, p. 310.

[37]Ibid., pp. 14-15. See footnote 30 this section for details about the popes of Abelard's school of thought.

[38]Sikes, Peter Abailard, p. 244. Abelard's successors relied on quotes to an even greater degree than did Abelard.

[39]Hawkins, A Sketch of Mediaeval Philosophy, p. 77.

[40]Ibid., p. 90. Hawkins compares this method to the modern style of "Giving first a definition of virtue in philosophical terms, and then its application to the moral order and to theological graces." For Abelard's students, virtues only existed when practiced with acts of charity. After discussing charity, they could talk of other virtues.

[41]Ibid., p. 91.

[42]Luscombe, The School of Peter Abelard, p. 5.

[43]Hawkins, A Sketch of Mediaeval Philosophy, p. 68.

[44]Haskins, The Rise of Universities, pp. 72-73.

[45]Hawkins, A Sketch of Mediaeval Philosophy, p. 61. Theologians began to "make theology a deductive science" with the aid of Aristotle's logical works.

[46]Ibid., p. 93.   [47]Ibid., p. 64.

[48]Ibid., p. 87. This is particularly noticeable in Abelard's Theologia Christiana and Scito te Ipsum. Ethics was described as derived from the mind of man, and the belief in the Trinity was said to have been known to oriental religions as

well as Greek philosophy. This search for a common link to the universality of morals and theology, which was begun by Abelard, was to be resumed
with diligence by the men of the eighteenth century Enlightenment in their explorations for a
natural law and a natural religion.

[49]Ibid., p. 65. Hawkins quotes from the letter that St. Bernard wrote to Henry Murdach, master at Paris:
   "Why do you seek in the written word the Word
   who is already here before your eyes, the Word
   made flesh? . . . The trees and the rocks will
   teach you that which you cannot hear from
   masters."

[50]Ibid., p. 89. The concept of his times was
based upon the act alone, and not the intention.
The difficulty involved determining the truth of
what one might call one's intention in a matter
subject to a judgment.

[51]Abelard, Abelard's Christian Theology, trans.
McCallum, p. 46.

[52]Otto of Freising, The Two Cities: A Chroni-
cle of Universal History to the Year 1146 A.D.,
trans. with an introduction and notes by Charles
Christopher Mierow. Records of Civilization.
Sources and Studies, no. 9 (New York: Columbia
University Press, 1926; reprint ed., New York:
Octagon Books, Inc., 1966), p. 44, from the intro-
duction.

[53]Abelard, Abelard's Christian Theology, trans.
McCallum, p. 55. Abelard references St. Augus-
tine's work Against Five Heresies:
   "Let us hear what Sibyl the prophetess says:
   'The Lord gave to men another Lord to worship';
   and again: 'Know thy Lord to be the Son of
   God.'"

[54]Ibid., p. 56. McCallum mentions in n. 3
that this inclusion of an oriental religion by

Abelard is "of interest both to Christian Philosophy and to Comparative Religion."

[55]Ibid., p. 52. In n. 2, McCallum states that
Abelard's source for Plato's concept was probably
Timaeus, which had been translated into Latin in
the early Middle Ages.

[56]Ibid., p. 49. Again, Abelard uses St. Augustine to support his theory, and cites Augustine's City of God (xxvi. 6), Five Heresies (chap.
vi), and de Trinitate (Bk. 8).

[57]Ibid., p. 50. [58]Ibid.

[59]Sikes, Peter Abailard, p. 157. This opinion was also held by William of St. Thierry and
Walter of Mortagne in his Epistola. Abelard was
accused of creating a distinction in the Godhead.

[60]Luscombe, The School of Peter Abelard, pp.
146-147. Luscombe cites several examples. One,
the Cambridge Commentator, claimed to be quoting
Abelard's spoken words when he listed the properties of the divine persons as the Father being
omnipotent, the Spirit being benign, "and benignity is no power," and the Son being "quaedam poten-
tia." Abelard replied that he never wrote such a
heresy and said in his defense that "it is not
proper to say that the Son . . . is a certain
power of God." Luscombe suggests that either Abelard was loosely quoted, or that he "lectured less
carefully than he wrote."

[61]Ibid., p. 172.

[62]Sikes, Peter Abailard, p. 245. Sikes included as examples of this the de Sacrament of
Hugh of St. Victor and the Summa Sententiarum of
Peter Lombard in which they criticized Abelard's
ideas on Original Sin and the omnipotence of God,
which seemed to be limited in Abelard's theology.
They adhered to traditional doctrines on these issues.

[63]Ibid., pp. 245-246.

[64]Ibid., p. 245. The Ransom Theory held that Christ's Incarnation was necessary to ransom the souls of men, which since Adam, were the rightful property of the devil. Abelard, however, stressed the love and example of Christ to be imitated by men.

[65]St. Bernard of Clairvaux, Letters, p. 321, Letter 240 to Guy of Castello. Bernard added that it was expedient for Guy of Castello, the Church, and Abelard himself to have silence imposed upon Abelard after Sens.

[66]Ibid., p. 321, Letter 241 to Cardinal Ivo. This was written in 1140 after the Council of Sens as a precaution against Abelard making his appeal to the pope. Bernard added that Abelard
". . . feels himself to be quite safe, because he boasts that he has disciples amongst the cardinals and clerics in Curia and supposes that they, whose judgement and condemnation he ought to fear, will defend him in his past and present error.

[67]Morison, The Life and Times of St. Bernard, pp. 317-318. The author quotes at length the letter St. Bernard wrote to Pope Innocent II and is also known as the Tractatus de Erroribus Abaelardi or Contra Errores Abelardi. Bruno Scott James did not include this letter in his previously cited work since he considered it more of a tract than a letter, and so reserved it for placement "among the treatises of St. Bernard." (St. Bernard of Clairvaux, Letters, p. 320).

[68]Abelard, Abelard's Christian Theology, trans. McCallum, p. 69. Abelard inserted his own theory of intention and thus assured himself of God's forgiveness for any mistakes in his book in advance by virtue of his own reasoning.

[69]Abelard, The Letters of Abelard and Heloise,

trans. Radice, p. 270, from Abelard's "Confession of Faith."

70Durant, The Age of Faith, p. 939.

CONCLUSION

From the start of his career in disputation,
Peter Abelard relished the excitement of the verbal battles over ideas. He was an advocate for
the awakening of reason, who saw himself as "a
true philosopher not of the world but of God" and
attempted to examine "the basis of our faith by
analogy with human reason."[1] His teaching spanned
the schools of Paris to the wilderness of Troyes
and finally back to Paris, with the only great in-
terruption being the ten to eleven years he spent
as Abbot of St. Gildas in Brittany. But upon his
return to Paris, Abelard reigned in triumph over
the minds of thousands of students, so that St.
Bernard lamented in a letter to Cardinal Stephen,
Bishop of Palestrina--after the Council of Sens--
that Abelard

> . . . had long been silent, but while he
> kept silence in Brittany he conceived
> sorrow, and now in France he has brought
> forth iniquity. He has come out of his
> hole like a twisting snake . . . Raw and
> inexperienced listeners hardly finished
> with their dialectics, and those who can
> hardly, so to speak, stand the first ele-
> ments of the faith, are introduced by
> him to the mystery of the Holy Trinity,
> to the Holy of Holies, to the chamber
> of the King, and to him who is 'shrouded
> with darkness.'[2]

Abelard was possessed of a flamboyant nature,
eager for any opportunity to display his talent
for dialectic. He was not one to withhold or con-
ceal his disdain for lesser minds, and thus he

127

antagonized his rivals who then waited for the chance to claim their revenge through ecclesiastical councils. Abelard was twice condemned, not for heretical propositions as such, but for daring to question.

The problem of universals which Abelard addressed early in his career was not a trivial matter. It required the consideration of the nature of abstract thought and, in turn, the existence and structure of fact so far as it could be known. As such, the question of universals opened the way to the study of philosophical logic and metaphysics.[3] Abelard provided the thrust for the scholastic flowering of the thirteenth century and the beginnings of a systematic and complete Christian philosophy. He was without a doubt a questioner and an innovator, but his outlook was always from the standpoint of a sincere Christian.

Many of Abelard's theological concepts, such as those concerning the importance of intention in morals and the subjective factor in sin, were accepted by later generations. He was impeded in his endeavor to develope a systematic understanding of faith by his own intolerance for the ignorance of others and his contempt for what he considered the intellectual simplicity of his detractors. And yet, what Peter the Venerable said of Abelard's short stay at Cluny where his life came to an end may be applied to Abelard's place in history: he

> . . . is often and ever to be named
> and honoured as the servant and true
> philosopher of Christ . . . whom . . .
> enriched . . . (us) in his person with
> a gift more precious than any gold or
> topaz.[4]

CONCLUSION FOOTNOTES

[1]Abelard, The Letters of Abelard and Heloise, trans. Radice, pp. 77-78 passim (Hist. Cal.).

[2]St. Bernard of Clairvaux, Letters, p. 324, Letter 243.

[3]Hawkins, A Sketch of Mediaeval Philosophy, p. 41.

[4]Abelard, The Letters of Abelard and Heloise, trans. Radice, p. 281, Letter 115, from Peter the Venerable to Heloise (c. 1143). This letter is numbered from the collection by Constable, The Letters of Peter the Venerable op. cit.

APPENDIX A

LIST OF WORKS OF PETER ABELARD

1. Logica Ingredientibus (Logic for Beginners).
   Glosses on Porphyry, Categories, De Interpretatione (c. 1113-1120).

2. Introductiones Parvulorum (Commentaries on
   Little Treatises). (c. pre-1121).

3. Nostrorum petitioni sociorum (Written in
   Response to the Request of Our Friends).
   Glossulae super Popyrim (Second Commentary
   on Porphyry) (post 1120).

4. De unitate et Trinitate divina (On the Unity
   and Trinity of God) (c. 1120).

5. Sic et Non (Yes and No). 156 questions, pro
   and contra (c. 1122-1123).

6. Dialectica (Dialectic). (post 1121-1125).

7. Theologia Christiana (Christian Theology).
   (c. 1123-1124).

8. Introductio ad Theologian (Introduction to
   Theology). One of an intended three parts
   of a work Abelard referred to as the
   Theologia. Part I is Book 1 and 2 of the
   Introductio; Part II is Book 3, and is in-
   complete. Book 1 and 2 (c. 1124-1125);
   Book 3 (c. 1136+).

9. Expositio in Epistulam ad Romanos (Commentary
   on St. Paul's Letter to the Romans).

131

(post 1125).

10. Scito te Ipsum (Know Thyself or Ethics).
    (c. 1125-1138).

11. Historia Calamitatum (Story of My Misfor-
    tunes). (c. 1132-1135).

12. Letters to Heloise (if not forgeries)
    (c. 1135+).

13. Expositio in Hexameron (Commentary on the Six
    Days of Creation) (c. 1135).

14. Monitum (Reminders). Advice to his son As-
    tralabe. (c. 1135-1141).

15. Apologia. To St. Bernard, denying that he
    had committed any heresy in his writings.
    (c. 1141-1142).

16. Dialogue inter Philosophum, Judaeum et Chris-
    tianum (Dialogue Between a Philosopher, a
    Jew and a Christian) unfinished. (c.
    1141-1142).

17. "Confession of Faith." Cited by Berengar of
    Poitiers. (c. 1141-1142).

18. 34 short sermons, 93 hymns and several
    prayers created for the sisters at the
    Paraclete; and 6 laments (The Planctus).

APPENDIX B

LETTER OF PETER ABELARD, ABBOT OF ST. GILDAS, TO BERNARD, ABBOT OF CLAIRVAUX (c. 1129-1135)

This letter began with an appropriate greeting and recounted with how much pleasure the nuns of the Paraclete had enjoyed Bernard's visit, but then Abelard proceeded to demonstrate why the nuns should use the Lord's Prayer as rendered in St. Matthew rather than the commonly-used insertion from St. Luke which altered the "super-substantial bread" of Matthew to the "daily bread" of Luke. St. Gregory was cited as an authority to support Abelard's preference and then Abelard commenced a stinging attack against the practices of the Cistercians. Abelard wrote:

> . . . You Cistercians, indeed, are so vehement in your adherence to such a course, that you keep it and defend it against the practice of all the churches. You, forsooth, novel upstarts, and not a little proud of your novelty, have decided on celebrating the Holy Office in a way opposed to the ancient, universal, and long-standing custom whether of monks or clerks. And yet you do not expect to be blamed if this novelty or singularity of yours differs from antiquity, so long as you consider it consonant with reason and the tenor of the Rule; neither do you care for the wonder and objections of others, provided you follow what you think are your reasons. By your leave, I will mention one or two points: you have rejected

133

the common hymns, and introduced others unheard of by us, unknown to the churches, and inferior also. Thus, throughout the year, at the vigils, whether of holidays or festivals, you are content with one and the same hymn, whereas the Church, according to the diversity of festivals and holidays, uses different hymns and psalms, and whatever else pertains to these, as common sense dictates. Hence those who hear you, whether at Christmas, Easter, or Pentecost, singing alsways the same hymn-- i.e. 'Aeterne rerum conditor'--are filled with the utmost astonishment, and moved less to admiration than derision. Those prayers which follow the supplication and the Lord's Prayer in every church, and the suffragia sanctorum, you have entirely prohibited, as if the world were not in need of your prayers, nor you of the intercession of the saints.[1]

---

[1]Morison, The Life and Times of Saint Bernard, pp. 279-280.

APPENDIX C

LETTER OF BERNARD OF CLAIRVAUX

TO POPE INNOCENT II (c. 1140)

This letter was essentially a treatise against Abelard's errors, and is quoted in part in Morison's <u>The Life and Times of Saint Bernard</u>, pages 317-318.

It is not wonderful if a man who cares not what his words may mean should rush in upon the hidden things of faith, and thus profanely invade and despoil the concealed treasures of devotion, seeing that he has no feeling either of piety or allegiance to the faith. At the very commencement of his 'Theology.' or rather Fool-ology, he defines faith as being opinion. As if any one might think or say what pleased him concerning it; or as if the sacraments of our faith, instead of reposing on certain truth, depended without certitude on wandering and various opinion, and rested not upon most undoubted truth. If the faith is unstable, is not our hope in vain? Therefore the martyrs were foolish to endure such torments for an uncertainty; for the sake of a doubtful reward, to pass through a painful death into everlasting exile. But God forbid that we should think as <u>he</u> does, that there is anything in our faith or hope which hangs on a doubtful opinion. Rather let us hold that the whole of it is grounded on certain, solid truth, preached divinely by oracles

135

and miracles, established and consecrated
by the childbirth of the Virgin, by the
blood of the Redeemer, by the glory of the
resurrection. These testimonies have been
made too credible for us to doubt them;
and if they fail in any way, 'the Spirit
beareth witness with our spirit, that we
are the children of God.' How then can
any one dare to call faith opinion, except
it be one who hath not yet received that
Spirit, or ignores or disbelieves the Gos-
pel? 'I know,' exclaims the Apostle,
'whom I have believed, and I am certain;'
and you whisper to me, 'Faith is opinion.'
You gabble on, and pretend that to be
doubtful than which nothing can be more
certain. Differently indeed writes St.
Augustine: 'Faith,' he says, 'dwelleth in
a man's heart, not by guessing and thinking, but by certain knowledge, conscience
bearing witness.' God forbid, therefore,
that Christian faith should have these
limits! These ideas and opinions belong
to the Academics, who doubt of all things
and know nothing. Therefore I walk safely,
following the Apostle of the Gentiles; and
I know I shall not be confounded. His
definition of faith, I confess, pleases
me: 'Faith is the substance of things
hoped for, the evidence of things not
seen.' 'The substance of things hoped
for,' he says, not the phantasies of empty
conjectures. You hear, 'the substance.'
You may not think or dispute on the faith
as you please; you may not wander here and
there, through the wastes of opinion, the
by-ways of error. By the name 'substance'
something certain and fixed is placed before you; you are enclosed within certain
boundaries, you are restrained within un-
changing limits. For faith is not an
opinion, but a certitude.

APPENDIX D

THE APOLOGY FOR ABELARD BY BERENGAR OF POITIERS

(c. 1140)

The Apology for Abelard was written by Berengar of Poitiers after the Council of Sens (1140),
and is quoted in part by Morison, The Life and
Times of Saint Bernard, pages 314-316.

> The renown of your fame, O Bernard, causes
> copies of your writings to be spread
> abroad everywhere. It is no marvel that
> they are placed upon the stage of popular-
> ity, seeing that, whatever they are, they
> are approved by the great ones of the
> present day. People wonder to see in you,
> a man ignorant of the liberal arts, such
> fertility of eloquence; so that your pro-
> ductions have covered the surface of the
> earth. To such persons the answer is,
> that 'Great are the works of the Lord.'
> But there is no reason why they should
> wonder; indeed the wonder would be greater
> if you lacked flowing words. For we hear
> that from your earliest youth you composed
> comic songs and polished verses. Do you
> not remember how you strove to surpass
> your brothers in rhythmical contests, and
> in the subtlety of invention? And was it
> not especially painful to you to meet with
> any one who could answer you with impu-
> dence equal to your own? . . .
> Happy did we deem these modern times
> in being lit up by such a brilliant star,
> and we considered that a world doomed to

perdition was supported only by your merits. We believed that on the words of
your mouth depended the mercy of Heaven,
the temperature of the air, the fertility
of the earth, and the blessing of the
fruits thereof. We thought the very
devils roared at your commands, and we
gloried in our fortune in having such a
patron.

Now alas! what was hidden is revealed;
you have awakened the sting of the sleep-
ing snake. Neglecting everything else,
you have placed Peter Abelard as a target
for your arrows, on whom you might vomit
forth the poison of your wrath. By your
collection of bishops at Sens you pro-
nounced him a heretic, you cut him off
from his mother the Church. Whilst he was
walking in the way of Christ, like a mur-
derer rushing from an ambush, you have
despoiled him of the seamless coat; you
harangued the people, bidding them to pray
to God for him, while in private you took
means to get him proscribed by the Christian world . . .

After dinner Peter's book was brought
in, and somebody was told to read it in a
loud voice. The fellow, full of hatred to
Peter, watered by the vine--not of Him who
said 'I am the true vine,' but of that
which cast the patriarch naked on the
ground--bellowed out louder than he was
asked to do. Presently you saw the pontiffs insult him (i.e. Peter), applaud
with their feet, laugh, and play the fool,
so that any one might see they were paying
their vows not to Christ, but to Bacchus.
Then the cups were saluted, the goblets
filled, the wine praised, the episcopal
throats moistened. Horace's recommenda-
tion,

> 'Nunc est bibedum nunc pede libero,
> Pulsanda tellus,' (Drinking sets
> the foot free to strike the
> earth.)

138

was executed from memory. But their po-
tations of the sleepy fluid had already
drowned the hearts of the pontiffs.
When, during the reading, anything subtle
or divine, but unusual to pontifical ears,
was heard, they were all of them cut to
the heart, and gnashed their teeth at
Peter; and these moles, judging a philosopher, exclaimed, 'Shall we suffer this
wretch to live?' Wagging their heads, as
did the Jews, they said, 'Ah! behold him
who destroyeth the temple of God.' So did
the blind judge words of light; so did
drunkards condemn a sober man; so did eloquent wine-cups attack the organ of the
Trinity . . . These great philosophers had
filled with wine their barrels of throats.
The fumes of it had so invaded their
brains, that the eyes of all were drooping
from sleep. Still the reader droned on;
the assembly snored. One rested on his
elbow, another procured a cushion, a third
took his nap with his head upon his knees.
So when the reader came upon some thorn-
bush in Peter's field, he exclaimed to the
deaf ears of the bishops, 'Damnatis?'
(do you damn this?) Hardly awake at the
last syllable, in a drowsy voice, and with
hanging heads, they muttered 'Damnaus.'
Others, however, roused by the noise of
the damners, decapitated the word, and
said . . . 'namus.'

APPENDIX E

ABELARD'S CONFESSION OF FAITH (c. 1140)

Abelard's "Confession of Faith" was included
in Berengar's Apology for Abelard but was omitted
from the Morison extract. It is quoted alone in
Abelard, The Letters of Abelard and Heloise,
trans. Radice, pages 270-271, and was addressed
to Heloise. Berengar claimed the "Confession of
Faith" was a fragment, but Radice believes it may
be complete.

> Heloise my sister, once dear to me in the
> world, now dearest to me in Christ, logic
> has made me hated by the world. For the
> perverted, who seek to pervert and whose
> wisdom is only for destruction, say that I
> am supreme as a logician, but am found
> wanting in my understanding of Paul. They
> proclaim the brilliance of my intellect
> but detract from the purity of my Chris-
> tian faith. As I see it, they have
> reached this judgement by conjecture rath-
> er than weight of evidence. I do not wish
> to be a philosopher if it means conflict-
> ing with Paul, nor to be an Aristotle if
> it cuts me off from Christ. For there is
> no other name under heaven whereby I must
> be saved. I adore Christ who sits on the
> right hand of the Father. I embrace in
> the arms of faith him who acts divinely in
> the glorious flesh of a virgin which he
> assumed from the Paraclete. And so, to
> banish fearful anxiety and all uncertain-
> ties from the heart within your breast,
> receive assurance from me, that I have

founded my conscience on that rock on
which Christ built his Church. What is
written on the rock I will testify briefly.
    I believe in the Father, the Son, and
the Holy Spirit; the true God who is one
in nature; who comprises the Trinity of
persons in such a way as always to preserve Unity in substance. I believe the
Son to be co-equal with the Father in all
things, in eternity, power, will and
operation. I do not hold with Arius, who
is driven by perverted intellect or led
astray by demonic influence to introduce
grades into the Trinity, laying down that
the Father is greater, and the Son less
great, forgetting the injunction of the
Law, 'You shall not mount up to my altar
by steps.' He mounts up to the altar of
God by steps who assigns first and second
place in the Trinity. I bear witness that
in everything the Holy Spirit is consub-
stantial and co-equal with the Father and
the Son, and is he who, as my books often
declare, is known by the name of Goodness.
I condemn Sabellius, who, in holding that
the person of the Father is the same as
that of the son, asserts that the Passion
was suffered by the Father--hence his followers are called Patripassiani.
    I believe that the Son of God became
the Son of Man in such a way that one person is of and in two natures; that after
he had completed the mission he had under-
taken in becoming man he suffered and died
and rose again, and ascended to heaven
whence he will come to judge the living
and the dead. I also declare that in
baptism all offences are remitted, and
that we need grace whereby we may begin on
good and preserve in it, and that having
lapsed we may be restored through peni-
tence. But what need have I to speak of
the resurrection of the body? I would
pride myself on being a Christian in vain

141

if I did not believe that I would live
again.

This then is the faith on which I
rest, from which I draw my strength in
hope. Safely anchored on it, I do not
fear the barking of Scylla, I laugh at
the whirlpool of Charybdis, and have no
dread of the Sirens' deadly songs. The
storm may rage but I am unshaken, though
the winds may blow they leave me unmoved;
for the rock of my foundation stands firm.[1]

---

[1]Reprinted by permission of Penguin Books, Ltd.

APPENDIX F

TWO HYMNS BY ABELARD FOR THE

BREVIARY OF THE PARACLETE

Vespers: Saturday Evening

How mighty are the Sabbaths,
    How mighty and how deep,
That the high courts of heaven
    To everlasting keep.
What peace unto the weary,
    What pride unto the strong,
When God in Whom are all things
    Shall be all things to men.

Jerusalem is the city
    Of everlasting peace,
A peace that is surpassing
    And utter blessedness;
Where finds the dreamer waking
    Truth beyond dreaming far,
Nor there the heart's possessing
    Less than the heart's desire.

But the courts of heaven
    And Him who is the King,
The rest and the refreshing,
    The joy that is therein,
Let those that know it answer
    Who in that bliss have part,
If any word can utter
    The fullness of the heart.

But ours, with minds uplifted
    Unto the heights of God,
With our whole heart's desiring,
    To take the homeward road,
And the long exile over,
    Captive in Babylon,
Again unto Jerusalem,
    To win at last return.

There, all vexation ended,
    And from all grieving free,
We sing the song of Zion
    In deep security,
And everlasting praises
    For all Thy gifts of grace
Rise from Thy happy people,
    Lord of our blessedness.

There Sabbath unto Sabbath
    Succeeds eternally,
The joy that has no ending
    Of souls in holiday.
And never shall the rapture
    Beyond all mortal ken
Depart the etenal chorus
    That angels sing with men.

Now to the King Eternal
    Be praise eternally,
From whom are all things, by whom
    And in whom all things be.
From Whom, as from the Father,
    By Whom, as by the Son,
In Whom, as in the Spirit,
    God the Lord, Three in One.

Good Friday: The Third Nocturn

Alone to sacrifice Thou goest, Lord,
Giving Thyself to death whom Thou wilt slay,
For us Thy wretched folk is any word,
Whose sins have brought Thee to this agony?

For they are ours, O Lord, our deeds, our deeds.
Why must Thou suffer torture for our sin?
Let our hearts suffer for Thy passion, Lord,
That very suffering may Thy mercy win.

This is that night of tears, the three days'
     space,
Sorrow abiding of the eventide,
Until the day break with the risen Christ,
And hearts that sorrowed shall be satisfied.

So may our hearts share in Thine anguish, Lord,
That they may sharers of Thy glory be:
Heavy with weeping may the three days pass,
To win the laughter of Thine Easter Day.

Translated by Helen Waddell, Mediaeval Latin
Lyrics, (W.W. Norton and Company, Inc., 1889;
reprint ed., 1977), pp. 163-167.

APPENDIX G

ONE LAMENT FROM THE PLANCTUS BY ABELARD

David's Lament for Jonathan

Low in thy grave with thee
    Happy to lie,
Since there's no greater thing left Love to do;
    And to live after thee
Is but to die,
    For with but half a soul what can Life do?

So share thy victory,
    Or else thy grave,
Either to rescue thee, or with thee lie;
    Ending that life for thee,
That thou didst save,
    So Death that sundereth might bring more nigh.

Peace, O my striken lute!
    Thy strings are sleeping.
Would that my heart could still
    Its bitter weeping!

_____

Translated by Waddell, Mediaeval Latin Lyrics,
p. 169.

BIBLIOGRAPHY

Primary Sources

(ABELARD, Peter and Heloise.) The Letters of Abe-
    lard and Heloise. Translated by C.K. Scott
    Moncrief. New York: Alfred A. Knopf, 1933.

_____. The Letters of Abelard and Heloise.
    Translated by Betty Radice. New York: Penguin
    Books, 1976 by permission of Penguin Books, Ltd

ABAELARDUS, Petrus. Dialectica. Edited with an
    introduction by L.M. DeRijk. 2nd revised ed.
    Netherlands: Van Gorcum and Company, 1970.

(ABELARD, Peter.) Abelard's Christian Theology.
    Translated by J. Ramsay McCallum. Oxford:
    B.H. Blackwell, 1948; reprint ed., Merrick,
    New York: Richwood Publishing Company, 1976.

ABELARD, Peter. Ethics. Translated with an in-
    troduction and notes by David Edward Luscombe.
    Oxford: The Clarendon Press, 1971.

_____. The Story of Abelard's Adversities. A
    Translation with Notes of the Historia Calami-
    tatum. Translated by J. T. Muckle. Preface
    by Étienne Gilson. Toronto, Canada: The
    Pontifical Institute of Mediaeval Studies,
    1964.

_____. The Story of My Misfortunes, The Autobiog-
    raphy of Peter Abelard. Translated by Henry

Adams Bellows. Introduction by Ralph Adams Cram. New York: Macmillan Publishing Company, Inc., 1922.

_____. Bernard of Clairvaux. His Life as Recorded in the Vita Prima Bernardi by William of St. Thierry, Arnold of Bonnevaux, Geoffrey and Philip of Clairvaux, and Odo of Deuil. Translated by Adrian Walker and Geoffrey Webb. London: A. R. Mowbray and Company, Ltd., 1959.

_____. Bernard of Clairvaux: Studies Presented to Dom Jean Leclerq. Cistercian Studies Series, No. 23. Washington, D. C.: Cistercian Publications, Consortium Press; Cistercian Publications, Inc., Kalamazoo, Michigan, 1973.

BERNARD of Clairvaux. The Letters of St. Bernard of Clairvaux. Translated by Bruno Scott James. London: Burns, Oates and Washbourne, Ltd., 1953.

BURCH, George Bosworth. Early Medieval Philosophy. New York: King's Crown Press, Columbia University, 1951.

GUIBERT of Nogent. Self and Society in Medieval France. The Memoirs of Abbot Guibert of Nogent (1064?-c. 1125). Translated with an introduction by John F. Benton. Harper Torchbooks. New York: Harper and Row, 1970.

JOHN of Salisbury. John of Salisbury's Memoirs of the Papal Court. Translated by Marjorie Chibnall. London: Thomas Nelson and Sons, Ltd., 1956; reprint ed. 1965.

JOHN of Salisbury. The Metalogicon, A Twelfth Century Defense of the Verbal and Logical Arts of the Trivium. Translated with an introduction and notes by Daniel D. McGarry. Berkeley: University of California Press, 1962.

_____. The Statesman's Book of John of Salisbury. Translated by John Dickinson. New York: Russell and Russell, 1963.

MC KEON, Richard, ed. and trans. Selections From Medieval Philosophy, Vol. I, Augustine to Albert the Great. New York: Charles Scribner's Sons, 1929; renewal copyright 1957.

MORISON, James Cotter. The Life and Times of Saint Bernard, Abbot of Clairvaux A.D. 1091-1153. London: Macmillan and Company, 1877.

OTTO of Freising and His Continuator Rahewin. The Deeds of Frederick Barbarossa. Translated and annotated with an introduction by Charles Christopher Mierow. New York: W.W. Norton and Company, Inc., 1966.

_____. The Two Cities: A Chronicle of Universal History to the Year 1146 A.D. Translated with an introduction and notes by Charles Christopher Mierow. Records of Civilization. Sources and Studies, no. 9. New York: Columbia University Press, 1926; reprint ed. New York: Octagon Books, Inc., 1966.

(PETER the Venerable.) The Letters of Peter the Venerable. Edited by Giles Constable. 2 Vols. with an introduction and notes by Giles Constable. Cambridge, Massachusetts: Harvard University Press, 1967.

SHAPIRO, Herman, ed. Medieval Philosophy, Selected Readings from Augustine to Buridan. The Modern Library. New York: Random House, Inc., 1964.

TIERNEY, Brian, ed. The Middle Ages. Vol. I: Sources of Medieval History. 2nd ed. New York: Alfred A. Knopf, Publisher, 1973.

WADDELL, Helen. Mediaeval Latin Lyrics. New York: W.W. Norton and Company, Inc. 1889; reprint ed., 1977.

Secondary Sources

CARRÉ, Meyrick Heath. <u>Realists and Nominalists</u>.
London: Oxford University Press, 1961.

CLAGETT, Marshall; POST, Gaines; REYNOLDS, Robert,
eds. <u>Twelfth Century Europe and the Founda-
tions of Modern Society</u>: HOLMES, Urban T.
<u>Transitions in European Education</u>. Madison,
Wisconsin: University of Wisconsin Press,
1966.

COMPAYRÉ, Gabriel. <u>Abelard and the Origin and
Early History of Universities</u>. New York:
Greenwood Press, Publishers, 1949.

DELHAYE, Philippe. <u>Medieval Christian Philosophy</u>.
Translated by S.J. Tester. Vol. 12 of the
<u>Twelfth Century Encyclopedia of Catholicism</u>,
section 1; Knowledge and Faith. New York:
Hawthorne Books, Publishers, 1960.

DE WULF, Maurice Marie Charles Joseph. <u>History of
Medieval Philosophy</u>. Vol. 1: <u>From the Beginnings to the End of the Twelfth Century</u>. 6th
ed. Translated by Ernest C. Messenger. New
York: Dover Publications, Inc., 1952.

DURANT, Will. <u>The Story of Civilization</u>. Vol.
IV: <u>The Age of Faith</u>. New York: Simon and
Schuster, 1950.

GILSON, Étienne. <u>Reason and Revelation in the
Middle Ages</u>. New York: Charles Scribner's
Sons, 1938.

_____. <u>The Spirit of Mediaeval Philosophy</u>. Trans-
lated by A.H.C. Downes. New York: Charles
Scribner's Sons, 1940.

HASKINS, Charles Homer. <u>The Rise of Universities</u>.
Brown University, The Colver Lectures. New
York: Henry Holt and Company, 1923.

HAWKINS, D.J.B. _A Sketch of Mediaeval Philosophy_.
New York: Greenwood Press, Publishers, 1968.

KNOWLES, David. _The Evolution of Medieval
Thought_. Baltimore: Helicon Press, 1962.

LEFF, Gordon. _Medieval Thought. St. Augustine to
Ockham_. Baltimore: Penguin Books, 1958.

LLOYD, Roger B. _The Striken Lute, An Account of
the Life of Peter Abelard_. Port Washington,
New York: Kennikat Press, 1932.

LUSCOMBE, David Edward. _The School of Peter Abelard - The Influence of Abelard's Thought in
the Early Scholastic Period_. Cambridge:
Cambridge University Press, 1969.

MC CABE, Joseph. _Peter Abelard_. New York: G. P.
Putnam's Sons, 1901.

MAURER, Armand Augustine. _Medieval Philosophy_.
Gen. ed. Étienne Gilson. New York: Random
House, 1962.

MERTON, Thomas. _The Last of the Fathers. Saint
Bernard of Clairvaux and the Encyclical
Letter, "Doctor Mellifluus"_. New York: Har-
court, Brace and Company, 1954.

SIKES, J.G. _Peter Abailard_. Cambridge: The University Press, 1932; reprint ed., New York:
Russell and Russell, Inc., 1965.

VIGNAUX, Paul. _Philosophy in the Middle Ages, An
Introduction_. Translated by E.C. Hall. New
York: Meridian Books, Inc., 1959.

WADDELL, Helen. _The Wandering Scholars_. London:
Constable and Company, Ltd., 1927; revised
and reprinted ed., 1966.